marie claire

hot

Published by Murdoch Books Pty Limited.

Murdoch Books Australia
Pier 8/9, 23 Hickson Rd
Millers Point NSW 2000
Phone: +61 (0)2 8220 2000
Fax: +61 (0)2 8220 2558

Murdoch Books UK Limited
Erico House, 6th Floor North
93–99 Upper Richmond Road
Putney, London SW15 2TG
Phone: +44 (0)20 8785 5995
Fax: +44 (0)20 8785 5985

Author and Stylist: Michele Cranston
Photographer: Petrina Tinslay
Design manager: Vivien Valk
Concept and design: Lauren Camilleri
Editor: Gordana Trifunovic
Food preparation: Ross Dobson and Jo Glynn
Production: Adele Troeger

Chief executive: Juliet Rogers
Publisher: Kay Scarlett

National Library of Australia Cataloguing-in-Publication Data
Cranston, Michele. Marie Claire hot. Includes index.
ISBN 1 74045 671 8.
1. Cookery. I. Title. II. Title: Marie Claire (North Sydney, N.S.W.). 641.5

Printed by 1010 Printing International Ltd. Printed in China. First printed 2005.

Important: Those who might be at risk from the effects of salmonella poisoning (the elderly,
pregnant women, young children and those suffering from immune deficiency diseases) should
consult their doctor with any concerns about eating raw eggs.
Conversion guide: You may find cooking times vary depending on the oven you are using. For
fan-forced ovens, as a general rule, set the oven temperature to 20°C (35°F) lower than indicated
in the recipe. We have used 20 ml (4 teaspoon) tablespoon measures. If you are using a
15 ml (3 teaspoon) tablespoon, for most recipes the difference will not be noticeable. However, for
recipes using baking powder, gelatine, bicarbonate of soda (baking soda) or small amounts of flour
and cornflour, add an extra teaspoon for each tablespoon specified.

marie claire
hot

michele cranston
photography by petrina tinslay

MURDOCH BOOKS

contents

hot introduction

Welcome to *marie claire hot*, a selection of our favourite recipes that are warm and inviting, hot and spicy, rich and chocolatey or simply berry marvellous. A thick and hearty book with lots of yummy ideas which we hope will inspire you, with everything from simple tomato salads and chilli salsas through to warming stews and rich chocolate cakes.

I've had a lot of fun revisiting old favourites and I hope that you have as much fun cooking and eating from our selection.

michele cranston

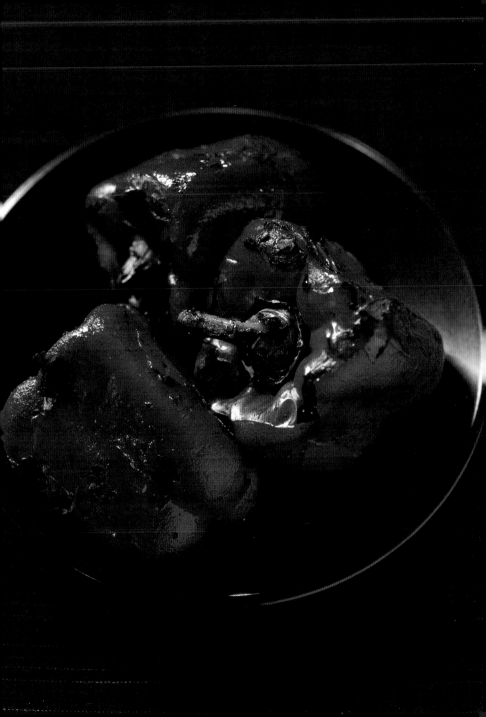

ingredient note # chillies

Hot and fiery, gently warming or only for the brave, chillies come in a range of shapes, sizes and colours, from the tiny bird's eye chilli through to small and large bell shapes and on to the large Mexican-style chillies.

When using fresh chillies, your choice of chilli is really a matter of personal taste depending upon your heat tolerance. Remember that the smaller the chilli the hotter it is. If you don't like too much bite then buy the large red chillies and always remove the seeds. However, it is always advisable to test a little of the chilli since even within the range of larger chillies the heat factor will vary. If you like your food hot, then the small bird's eye chillies are the ones for you, and if you're feeling particularly brave then leave the seeds intact. And remember that no matter how hot the chilli, always wash your hands after preparing them as a residue of the heat-inducing capsaicin will remain on your fingers long after you've finished slicing and chopping.

If you like heat and smoky flavours then investigate some of the dried and tinned Mexican chillies like the chipotle and ancho varieties.

There's nothing more disappointing than a cold and tasteless tomato. So remember these two basic rules — never store tomatoes in the refrigerator, and only use them when they are a rich, ruby red.

Nowadays, there is an inspiring range available in supermarkets and greengrocers and if not perfectly red then allow them a couple of days on your kitchen bench before using. Think cherry tomatoes, multicoloured teardrop tomatoes, baby and full-sized roma (plum) tomatoes, truss tomatoes and vine-ripened tomatoes.

To enhance the flavour of fresh tomatoes, you can simply toss them with some sea salt, torn basil leaves, black olives, salted capers, anchovies, oregano, bocconcini or wild rocket (arugula) leaves. Finish with a drizzle of extra virgin olive oil and some balsamic vinegar and you'll have created the perfect side to a summery meal. Though superb in salads, don't forget they also make a great base for salsas, sauces and casseroles.

ingredient note   # capsicums

Capsicums (peppers) are one of those wonderfully useful
vegetables that can appear in a surprising range of meals.
With their full spectrum of colours — red, yellow, orange and
green — they are the perfect vegetable when you want
to add a dash of colour to a recipe. When finely cut into
strips, they provide the perfect crunch factor in salads or
Asian stir-fries, and when finely chopped, they bring a
wonderful flavour to soups and sauces.

Baked whole and filled with a richly flavoured rice or meat
mixture, they're a satisfying mouthful of Mediterranean
comfort food. However, the red capsicums really come into
their own roasted or chargrilled. Once roasted, the flesh
becomes richly sweet and if chargrilled the additional
smokiness imparts a special background flavour to many
recipes. Roast red peppers can be puréed into a soup or dip,
tossed with fresh herbs as a salsa, marinated with fresh
herbs and garlic as part of a salad or antipasto plate, or
added to the ingredients of a fritatta or pizza.

berries

Sweet strawberries, luscious raspberries, juicy mulberries, fat blueberries and tart red currants ... who can say no to such a bowl of jewelled perfection? They can be served quite simply and still seem perfectly indulgent. Pile them into a bowl, sprinkle with a little sugar or dollop with some rich cream — desserts don't come much easier.

Berries and cream are a combination made in heaven. Serve strawberries with whipped cream and crushed meringue, or mash the berries with a little sugar and liqueur and pour over vanilla ice cream. Cut strawberries into quarters and put in a bowl with a dash of balsamic vinegar. Gently fold the vinegar through the berries. Spoon the strawberries over a large dollop of mascarpone cheese and drizzle with a little honey.

Berries freeze well so for a taste of summer in the cooler months invest in some frozen berries. They'll make a great jelly, crumble, sauce or can be folded through a basic cake mix for a rippled afternoon treat.

parmesan parchment bread chilli hushpuppies oven-roasted tomatoes radishes with butter and brown bread sautéed mushrooms seared beef with roasted tomato salsa grilled oysters fresh mozzarella salad poached tomato with goat's cheese chilli cornbread fried haloumi parcels tartlets with white bean purée and cherry tomatoes octopus on toast marinated olives tomato and basil bruschetta olive

01   starters and sides

and pine nut crostini baguette with grilled goat's cheese bocconcini and tomato in vine leaves cheese chilli and olive quesadillas mango salsa with black beans greek salad tomato with chilli and coriander tomato relish goat's curd prosciutto and sour

parmesan parchment bread

makes 8

20 g (³/₄ oz) butter
155 g (5¹/₂ oz/1 cup) finely chopped
 onion
1 teaspoon finely chopped rosemary
60 g (2¹/₄ oz/¹/₂ cup) plain (all-purpose)
 flour
2 tablespoons grated fresh parmesan
 cheese
caponata, to serve (basics)

Heat the butter in a small frying pan over medium heat. Add the onion and rosemary and cook, stirring, for 10 minutes, or until the onion is slightly caramelized. Remove from the heat, season with 1 teaspoon of salt and some freshly ground black pepper, and set aside to cool.

Preheat the oven to 150°C (300°F/ Gas 2). In a food processor, pulse the flour and parmesan until the mixture resembles breadcrumbs. Gradually add the onion mixture and process until the dough just comes together.

Divide the dough into eighths and roll out each portion very thinly between two sheets of well-floured baking paper. Remove the top sheet from each and place the dough on baking trays. Bake in batches for 10 minutes or until golden brown, then turn over and bake for an additional 5 minutes, or until crisp. Cool on a wire rack and break into pieces. Serve the parchment bread with caponata or a favourite dip.

marinated olives

makes 500 g (1 lb 2 oz)

500 g (1 lb 2 oz) mixed olives
4 long strips orange zest
2 garlic cloves, crushed
1 red chilli, seeded
a few thyme sprigs
3 tablespoons extra virgin olive oil

Put the olives in a bowl. Add the orange zest, garlic, chilli and thyme. Pour over the oil and toss to combine. Cover the olives and allow to marinate in the refrigerator overnight.

radishes with butter and brown bread
serves 6

1 ripe tomato
100 g (3¹/₂ oz) butter, softened
1 teaspoon sea salt
2 bunches small radishes
6 slices brown bread, to serve

Remove the seeds from the tomato and finely dice the flesh. Place in a bowl along with the softened butter and sea salt. Stir to combine and place into a small dish. Serve alongside the radishes with some thinly sliced brown bread.

fresh mozzarella salad

serves 4

4 x 125 g (4¹/2 oz) balls fresh
  mozzarella cheese
4 tablespoons virgin olive oil
120 g (4¹/4 oz) sage
20 large black olives, pitted
  and quartered
1 orange, zested and juiced

Cut the mozzarella into thick slices and arrange them on four plates.
Put the oil in a frying pan over high heat and add the sage leaves. As they begin to sizzle and darken, remove them from the oil and scatter them over the cheese. Gently pour a little of the oil over the mozzarella, then top with the olive quarters, orange zest and orange juice. Serve with toasted focaccia or ciabatta.

tomato and basil bruschetta

makes 8 pieces

8 ripe tomatoes
8 thick slices country-style bread
1 garlic clove, lightly crushed
a few basil leaves, torn
olive oil, to drizzle

Cut the tomatoes in half and scoop out most of the seeds. Discard the seeds and finely dice the flesh. Put the tomato into a bowl and season liberally with sea salt and freshly ground black pepper. Grill (broil) or toast the bread on both sides. Rub the top of each toasted slice with the garlic. Put the diced tomato onto the bread slices and top with torn basil leaves. Drizzle with olive oil and serve.

olive and pine nut crostini

makes 12 pieces

3 tablespoons red wine vinegar
6 anchovies
2 garlic cloves
115 g (4 oz/3/4 cup) pine nuts, toasted
2 teaspoons salted capers, rinsed
   and drained
4 hard-boiled egg yolks
12 large green olives, pitted
1 small handful flat-leaf (Italian) parsley,
   finely chopped
1 baguette, cut into 12 thin slices
olive oil
30 g (1 oz/1/4 cup) crumbled goat's
   cheese or shaved parmesan cheese

Preheat the oven to 150°C (300°F/ Gas 2). Put the vinegar, anchovy fillets, garlic, pine nuts, capers, egg yolks and olives into a food processor. Process to a smooth paste and spoon into a bowl. Add the parsley to the bowl. Brush one side of each baguette slice with olive oil. Put the slices on a baking tray and bake until golden brown, turning once. Spoon the topping onto the crostini slices and top with some crumbled goat's cheese or shaved parmesan cheese. Season with freshly ground black pepper.

seared beef and roasted tomato salsa crostini

makes 30 pieces

500 g (1 lb 2 oz) roma (plum) tomatoes, quartered
1 teaspoon sugar
10 basil leaves, shredded
10 mint leaves, shredded
1 teaspoon balsamic vinegar
300 g (10 1/2 oz) beef fillet, about 4 cm (1 1/2 in) in diameter
1 tablespoon vegetable oil
1 baguette, thinly sliced, to serve

Preheat the oven to 160°C (315°F/ Gas 2–3). Place the tomato quarters in a baking tin and sprinkle with the sugar and 1 teaspoon of salt. Bake for 40 minutes, or until the tomatoes begin to blacken at the edges and dry out. Remove from the heat and allow to cool. Slice the roasted tomatoes thinly and place in a bowl with the shredded basil and mint leaves. Add the balsamic vinegar and mix well to combine.

Season the beef fillet with freshly ground black pepper. Heat the oil in a frying pan over high heat and sear the fillet for 2 minutes on all sides. Remove from the heat and sprinkle with a little sea salt. Set aside to cool, then slice into 1 cm (1/2 in) widths. Place on the baguette slices and top with a little of the tomato salsa.

chilli cornbread

makes approximately 24 pieces

150 g (5½ oz/1 cup) polenta
125 g (4½ oz/1 cup) plain (all-purpose) flour
1 tablespoon baking powder
1 tablespoon sugar
3 eggs, lightly beaten
185 ml (6 fl oz/¾ cup) milk
2 tablespoons plain yoghurt
3 tablespoons olive oil
150 g (5½ oz/¾ cup) corn kernels
½ red capsicum (pepper), diced
1 small red chilli, seeded and chopped
3 teaspoons finely chopped marjoram
5 spring onions (scallions), thinly sliced
75 g (2½ oz/½ cup) grated mozzarella cheese

Place the polenta, flour, baking powder and sugar in a bowl. Make a well in the centre and add the eggs, milk, yoghurt and oil. Mix well. Add the corn, capsicum, chilli, marjoram and spring onions and mix well. Season with salt and pepper.

Preheat the oven to 180°C (350°F/ Gas 4). Pour the batter into a greased 30 x 20 cm (12 x 8 in) baking tray and top with the grated mozzarella. Bake for 35 minutes, or until a skewer comes out clean when inserted into the centre. Cool slightly in the tray, then turn out onto a board. Trim the sides and cut into 4 cm (1½ in) squares.

tartlets with white bean purée and cherry tomatoes

makes 30

100 g (3¹/₂ oz) dried white beans,
   soaked overnight
2 garlic cloves
30 cherry tomatoes
1¹/₂ tablespoons lemon thyme sprigs
125 ml (4 fl oz/¹/₂ cup) olive oil
30 pre-baked shortcrust tartlet
   cases (basics)

Drain the beans and place them and the garlic cloves in a saucepan filled with water. Bring to the boil and simmer for 30 minutes.

Meanwhile, preheat the oven to 180°C (350°F/Gas 4). Place the tomatoes in a baking tin with 2 teaspoons of the lemon thyme leaves, 60 ml (2 fl oz/¹/₄ cup) of olive oil and ¹/₂ teaspoon of salt. Bake for 30 minutes.

Add 2 teaspoons of salt to the white beans in the last 5 minutes of their cooking time. Check that the beans are soft, then drain. Mash by hand or in a food processor with the remaining olive oil and thyme. Season to taste with salt and freshly ground black pepper.

Fill each of the tart cases with a teaspoon of the white bean mash and top with one of the roasted cherry tomatoes. Serve immediately.

octopus on toast makes 32 pieces

8 small octopus, cleaned
2 tablespoons red wine vinegar
1 teaspoon dried oregano
250 ml (9 fl oz/1 cup) olive oil
8 thick slices white bread, crusts
  removed
4 garlic cloves
500 g (1 lb 2 oz) potatoes, boiled
  and mashed
1 tablespoon lemon juice
2 tablespoons finely chopped flat-leaf
  (Italian) parsley
1 tablespoon pitted and finely
  chopped black olives
2 teaspoons seeded and finely
  chopped red chilli
1 teaspoon finely chopped lemon zest

Place the octopus in a ceramic or glass bowl. Combine the vinegar, oregano and 60 ml (2 fl oz/1/4 cup) of the oil and pour over the octopus. Cover and leave to marinate for 30 minutes.

Preheat the oven to 180°C (350°F/ Gas 4). Cut each slice of bread into quarters. Place on a baking tray and toast in the oven until golden. Remove and allow to cool on a wire rack.

To make the sauce, place the garlic and 1 teaspoon of salt in a mortar and pestle and pound until soft and creamy. Place in a bowl and add the mashed potato and lemon juice. Whisk the mixture continuously while slowly adding the remaining olive oil. When the sauce is light and fluffy, fold in the parsley, olives, chilli and lemon zest.

Heat a heavy-based frying pan over high heat and sear the octopus for 2–3 minutes on both sides until coloured. Remove and cut into quarters. Place a heaped tablespoon of the sauce on each of the bread squares and top with the octopus.

fried haloumi parcels

makes 10 or 20

5 sheets filo pastry, cut in half to
   form squares
150 g (5½ oz) haloumi cheese
2 ripe tomatoes
80 g (2¾ oz) butter, melted
20 flat-leaf (Italian) parsley leaves
10 large mint leaves

Cover the pastry sheets with a damp cloth. Cut the haloumi into ten slices. Cut the tomatoes in half, then slice to form thin wedges. Lightly brush one of the sheets of filo with butter and fold in half to form a rectangle. Lightly butter the top, then place a slice of haloumi in the centre. Top with three wedges of tomato, two parsley leaves, a mint leaf and a sprinkle of ground black pepper. Fold the sides in on the haloumi and then roll up. Repeat the process with the remaining ingredients. Grease a large frying pan and cook the parcels over medium heat until the undersides are golden brown, then flip over to cook the other side. Serve warm, either whole or cut in half.

baguette with grilled goat's cheese

1 baguette
100 g (3¹/₂ oz) goat's cheese, sliced
dressed salad of baby leaves
1 handful olives
1 handful pomegranate seeds
4 marinated artichoke hearts, chopped

Slice the baguette on the diagonal into four long thin slices. Lightly toast the slices, then top with the goat's cheese. Grill (broil) until the cheese is golden brown. Serve on a dressed salad of baby leaves. Add the olives, pomegranate seeds and artichoke hearts. Season with freshly ground black pepper.

goat's curd, prosciutto and sour cherries on rye

makes 15 pieces

5 slices rye bread, crusts removed
100 g (3½ oz) goat's curd
5 slices prosciutto, each slice cut
    into three
60 g (2¼ oz/¼ cup) finely chopped
    bottled sour cherries

Cut each slice of bread into three fingers. Spread a little of the goat's curd onto each piece of bread and top with a piece of prosciutto and a teaspoon of chopped sour cherries. Serve immediately with a sprinkle of freshly ground black pepper.

grilled oysters   makes 24

40 g (1 1/2 oz) pancetta, finely diced
40 g (1 1/2 oz/1/2 cup) fresh breadcrumbs
2 tablespoons finely chopped flat-leaf
  (Italian) parsley
20 g (3/4 oz) unsalted butter, melted
1/2 teaspoon Tabasco sauce
1 tablespoon Worcestershire sauce
2 dozen rock oysters
lemon wedges, to serve

Place the pancetta, breadcrumbs and parsley in a small bowl and mix well. Pour on the melted butter, Tabasco sauce and Worcestershire sauce and fold through. Spread a teaspoon of the mixture over each of the oysters and place under a hot grill (broiler) for 2 minutes, or until the topping is golden brown. Remove from the heat and serve with wedges of lemon.

tomato salsa

serves 4

4 Roma (plum) tomatoes, thinly diced
10 basil leaves, thinly sliced
2 tablespoons finely diced red onion
1/2 teaspoon very finely chopped garlic
3 tablespoons extra virgin olive oil
1 tablespoon balsamic vinegar
1/2 teaspoon sea salt

Put the tomatoes into a bowl. Add the basil, onion, garlic, oil, balsamic vinegar and sea salt. Stir to combine. Check the seasoning; you may wish to add a little more salt to taste.

Serve with grilled tuna, blue-eye cod or swordfish. It can also be served with spicy marinated chicken or seared lamb.

mushroom and pancetta
bruschetta

makes 8 pieces

25 g (1 oz) butter
6 pieces pancetta, thinly sliced
200 g (7 oz) button mushrooms,
   thinly sliced
200 g (7 oz) oyster mushrooms,
   thinly sliced
8 thick slices country-style bread
1 garlic clove, lightly crushed
shaved parmesan cheese, to serve

Heat the butter in a frying pan over medium heat. As the butter melts, add the pancetta. Cook for 1 minute , then stir in the mushrooms. Cover the pan and reduce the heat to low. Allow the mushrooms to cook for a further 5 minutes, then remove from the heat. Season to taste with a little sea salt and freshly ground black pepper. Grill (broil) or toast the bread on both sides. Rub the top of each toasted slice with the garlic clove. Spoon the cooked mushrooms onto the bread slices. Top with the parmesan cheese.

cheese, chilli and olive quesadillas
makes 24 or 48 pieces

25 g (1 oz/1/4 cup) pitted black olives, chopped

1 large red chilli, seeded and chopped

125 ml (4 fl oz/1/2 cup) olive oil

320 g (111/4 oz/21/4 cups) mozzarella cheese, grated

150 g (51/2 oz/1 cup) feta cheese, grated

12 x 20 cm (8 in) tortillas

75 g (21/2 oz) coriander (cilantro) leaves

Preheat the oven to 180°C (350°F/ Gas 4). Place the olives, chilli and oil in a blender and blend to form a flavoured oil. Set aside. Place the grated mozzarella and feta in a bowl and toss to combine.

Place one of the tortillas on a baking tray. Sprinkle with a coating of the mixed cheeses, plus some coriander leaves. Cover with a second tortilla and brush well with the oil mixture. Continue making quesadillas with the remaining ingredients. Place on a baking tray and bake for 7 minutes. Turn the quesadillas over and cook for a further 7–8 minutes. Remove from the oven and slice into quarters or eighths. Serve immediately.

avocado with chilli salsa

serves 4

2 avocados

2 limes

1 tablespoon finely chopped red onion

8 cherry tomatoes, finely chopped

1 red chilli, seeded and finely chopped

1 tablespoon finely chopped coriander
  (cilantro) leaves

2 tablespoons extra virgin olive oil

1 teaspoon smoked paprika

1 handful coriander (cilantro) leaves

4 small white corn tortillas, toasted

Slice the avocados in half lengthways. Remove the seeds and scoop out the whole flesh with a large spoon. Put the avocados onto a plate and finely slice to form a fan. Squeeze half a lime over each avocado half and season with sea salt and freshly ground black pepper. Combine the onion, tomatoes, chilli and chopped coriander in a bowl then sprinkle over the avocado. Finish off with a drizzle of olive oil and a sprinkle of paprika. Garnish with the coriander leaves and serve with the toasted tortillas.

greek salad

serves 4

4 ripe tomatoes, cut into chunks
2 Lebanese (short) cucumbers,
  thickly cut
1/2 red onion, thinly sliced into
  paper-thin half rings
175 g (6 oz/1 cup) kalamata olives
1/4 teaspoon dried oregano
200 g (7 oz) creamy feta cheese,
  thickly sliced

dressing
1 teaspoon red wine vinegar
2–3 tablespoons extra virgin olive oil

Arrange the tomatoes on a serving platter. Add the cucumbers and onion. Scatter over the olives and sprinkle with the oregano. Put the feta slices on top of the salad. Combine the dressing ingredients and drizzle over the salad.

bocconcini and tomato in vine leaves

makes 24 parcels

24 packaged vine leaves
2 roma (plum) tomatoes, finely diced
200 g (7 oz) bocconcini (fresh baby
   mozzarella cheese), diced
24 large mint leaves
olive oil, for frying
lemon wedges, to serve

Unwrap the vine leaves and soak them for 1 hour in a large bowl filled with boiling water. Remove and gently pat dry. Place a row of tomato dice at one end of each vine leaf. Top with some of the bocconcini, a mint leaf and some freshly ground black pepper. Roll up firmly, folding the edges in as you go. Heat a large frying pan with a little oil and fry each of the parcels for 1 minute on each side. Serve warm with a squeeze of lemon.

tomato and cheese tarts

makes 6

8 roma (plum) tomatoes, cut into
   eight wedges
250 ml (9 fl oz/1 cup) thick
   (double/heavy) cream
3 eggs
150 g (5¹/2 oz/1 cup) grated gruyère
   cheese
150 g (5¹/2 oz/1¹/2 cups) grated
   parmesan cheese
6 pre-baked 8 cm (3¹/4 in) shortcrust
   tartlet cases (basics)
2 tablespoons oregano leaves
18 basil leaves, roughly torn
1 tablespoon extra virgin olive oil

Preheat the oven to 180°C (350°F/
Gas 4). Put the tomatoes on a baking
tray, sprinkle with salt and pepper
and bake for 30 minutes.

Whisk together the cream, eggs,
gruyère and parmesan. Pour the
mixture into the tart cases. Bake for
20 minutes, or until the eggs are set
and the filling is golden brown.

Put the tomatoes in a small bowl with
the oregano, basil and olive oil and
toss together. Pile the tomato mixture
on top of each tartlet. Serve as is or
on a bed of leafy greens.

prosciutto, mozzarella and tomato wraps

makes 20

2 roma (plum) tomatoes
20 thin slices prosciutto
200 g (7 oz) mozzarella cheese

Slice each tomato into ten vertical slices and then cut the slices in half horizontally. Lay a slice of prosciutto on the work surface. Place one halved slice of tomato on it, followed by a slice of mozzarella and then another slice of tomato. Season with freshly ground black pepper and roll up firmly to make a little parcel. Repeat with the remaining ingredients. Heat a lightly greased frying pan over medium heat and cook the prosciutto parcels for 2–3 minutes, or until golden brown.

grilled mushrooms   serves 4

8 field mushrooms
3 garlic cloves, finely chopped
1 teaspoon red chilli flakes
125 ml (4 fl oz/1/2 cup) extra virgin
   olive oil
8 slices ciabatta bread, toasted
150 g (51/2 oz) rocket (arugula)
1 handful flat-leaf (Italian) parsley
   leaves

Put the mushrooms, stalk side up, on a baking tray. Combine the garlic, chilli flakes and extra virgin olive oil in a small bowl. Spoon the flavoured oil over the mushrooms and season with a little sea salt.

Place under a hot grill (broiler) and cook for 10 minutes. Remove from the heat. Put the toasted ciabatta onto four serving plates. Add a few rocket leaves. Top with the warm mushrooms, scatter with the parsley and drizzle with the cooking liquid.

red and green sauce

makes 250 ml (9 fl oz/1 cup)

red sauce

500 g (1 lb 2 oz) roma (plum) tomatoes, quartered
1 teaspoon sugar
1 tablespoon pomegranate molasses
10 basil leaves
1 garlic clove
1 teaspoon ground cumin

Preheat the oven to 180°C (350°F/ Gas 4). Place the tomato pieces on a baking tray and sprinkle with the sugar and 1 teaspoon of salt. Roast for 40 minutes, or until the tomatoes are beginning to blacken at the edges and dry out. Place the tomatoes in a food processor or blender with the remaining ingredients and blend to form a smooth sauce. Season with salt and freshly ground black pepper.

green sauce

3 handfuls flat-leaf (Italian) parsley leaves
30 mint leaves
5 anchovies
1 tablespoon Indian lime pickle
3 teaspoons lemon juice
125 ml (4 fl oz/1/2 cup) olive oil

Place all the ingredients in a blender or food processor. Blend until smooth.

Note – These sauces can be used to accompany grilled lamb cutlets, and each is sufficient to serve with 10–12 cutlets. Serve both sauces at room temperature.

poached tomatoes with goat's cheese

serves 4

4 large vine-ripened tomatoes
1¹/₂ teaspoons sea salt
8 peppercorns
1 tablespoon balsamic vinegar
¹/₂ red onion, thinly sliced
6 sprigs parsley
100 g (3¹/₂ oz) rocket (arugula)
90 g (3¹/₄ oz/¹/₃ cup) pesto (basics)
115 g (4 oz/³/₄ cup) goat's cheese,
  crumbled

Preheat the oven to 180°C (350°F/ Gas 4). Put the tomatoes in a small, deep baking dish, then fill the dish with enough water to come halfway up the tomatoes. Add the sea salt, peppercorns, vinegar, onion and parsley sprigs and bake for 40 minutes.

Divide the rocket among four plates. Lift the tomatoes out of the dish, arrange on top of the rocket and drizzle each with some cooking liquid. Add some pesto and crumbled goat's cheese and serve.

tomatoes with chilli and coriander

serves 4

80 g (2³/₄ oz) coriander (cilantro) leaves, roughly chopped
1 red onion, finely diced
2 large red chillies, seeded and finely chopped
1 teaspoon sea salt
3 tablespoons olive oil
1 tablespoon balsamic vinegar
4 large ripe tomatoes

Put the coriander, onion, chillies, sea salt, olive oil and balsamic vinegar in a bowl and toss together.

Slice the tomatoes and arrange them on a plate. Scatter the coriander salsa on top, season and serve as a side dish or as a salad with a little seared tuna or fresh ricotta.

chilli hushpuppies　　makes 20

90 g (3¹/₄ oz/³/₄ cup) plain (all-purpose)
　flour
1 teaspoon baking powder
1 egg
20 g (³/₄ oz) butter, melted
3 tablespoons milk
1 teaspoon Tabasco sauce
2 corn cobs, kernels removed
　(approximately 400 g/14 oz/2 cups)
100 ml (3¹/₂ fl oz) vegetable oil

Place the flour, baking powder, egg, melted butter and ¹/₂ teaspoon of salt in a mixing bowl and stir together. Add the milk and Tabasco sauce to form a thick batter, then add the fresh corn. Heat the oil over medium heat in a frying pan. Drop small spoonfuls of the batter into the oil in batches and fry each side until golden brown. Remove and drain on paper towels. Serve warm with a sweet chilli sauce.

chilli pumpkin quesadillas

makes 20

50 g (1³/4 oz/¹/3 cup) pitted and chopped black olives
1 large red chilli, seeded and chopped
125 ml (4 fl oz/¹/2 cup) olive oil
500 g (1 lb 2 oz) pumpkin (winter squash)
1 teaspoon smoked paprika
300 g (10¹/2 oz/2 cups) grated mozzarella cheese
150 g (5¹/2 oz/1 cup) crumbled feta cheese
10 x 16 cm (6¹/4 in) white corn tortillas
90 g (3¹/4 oz) coriander (cilantro) leaves

Preheat the oven to 180°C (350°F/ Gas 4). Put the olives, chilli and oil into a blender and blend to form a flavoured oil. Dice the pumpkin into small pieces and put onto a baking tray. Brush with a little of the chilli oil. Sprinkle with the paprika. Bake for 30 minutes, or until golden brown and soft. Put the cheeses into a bowl and toss to combine.

Put one tortilla onto a clean board. Sprinkle with a liberal coating of the mixed cheeses, some of the roast pumpkin and a scattering of coriander leaves. Cover with a second tortilla, brush well with the flavoured oil and set aside. Repeat with the remaining ingredients. Put the quesadillas onto an oiled baking tray. Bake for 7 minutes. Turn over the quesadillas and cook for a further 7–8 minutes. Remove from the oven and slice into quarters. Serve.

tuna and red capsicum skewers

makes 20

500 g (1 lb 2 oz) tuna fillet
1 tablespoon olive oil
1 teaspoon ground coriander
2 teaspoons ground cumin
1 red capsicum (pepper)
20 small skewers, soaked in hot water
   for 20 minutes

lemon mayonnaise

2 egg yolks
1 lemon, zest grated, juiced
250 ml (9 fl oz/1 cup) vegetable oil
1 tablespoon finely chopped preserved
   lemon
1 tablespoon finely chopped coriander
   (cilantro) leaves
2 tablespoons lime juice

Cut the tuna into 2 cm (3/4 in) cubes and place in a bowl. Add the oil, ground coriander and cumin and mix through. Set aside and allow to marinate for 1 hour. Preheat the oven to 180°C (350°F/Gas 4).

To make the lemon mayonnaise, whisk the egg yolks, grated zest and lemon juice together in a bowl. Slowly drizzle in the oil, whisking the mixture until it becomes thick and creamy. Season with salt and white pepper. Place the mayonnaise in a small bowl and stir in the preserved lemon, coriander leaves and lime juice.

Slice the capsicum into 2 cm (3/4 in) squares and then skewer on two alternate pieces of tuna and capsicum per skewer. Place on a baking tray and bake for 5–7 minutes. Season with salt and freshly ground black pepper. Serve with the lemon mayonnaise.

mango salsa with black beans

serves 4

170 g (6 oz) tin Chinese black beans
1 mango, diced
1 teaspoon ground cumin
1 large red chilli, seeded and
  finely chopped
3 tablespoons lime juice
1 teaspoon sesame oil
2 spring onions (scallions), thinly sliced
1 large handful coriander (cilantro)
`leaves

Rinse the black beans, drain them and put them in a large bowl. Add the remaining ingredients, stir to combine and season to taste. Serve with barbecued chicken or as a side salad.

tomato relish

makes 750 ml (26 fl oz/3 cups)

1.5 kg (3 lb 5 oz) tomatoes, coarsely
  chopped
1 red onion, thinly sliced
3 garlic cloves, finely chopped
1 tablespoon finely grated fresh ginger
1/2 teaspoon ground allspice
2 teaspoons yellow mustard seeds
1/4 teaspoon red chilli powder
2 teaspoons sea salt
200 ml (7 fl oz) white wine vinegar
250 g (9 oz/scant 1 1/4 cups) sugar

Put the tomatoes, onion, garlic, ginger, allspice, mustard seeds, chilli powder, sea salt and white wine vinegar into a large pot. Bring to the boil. Simmer, covered, for 1 hour before adding the sugar. Continue to simmer, uncovered, for 40 minutes, stirring occasionally. Pour into sterilized jars and allow to cool before storing. Serve as a condiment on ham or cheddar sandwiches or spooned over sliced leg ham or grilled lamb.

roasted red capsicums serves 2

4 red capsicums (peppers)
2 tablespoons olive oil

Preheat the oven to 200°C (400°F/ Gas 6). Place a small rack on or over a baking tray or roasting tin. Lightly rub the capsicums with olive oil and place on the rack. Bake until the skin begins to blister and blacken. Turn the capsicums several times so that the skin blisters all over.

Remove the capsicums from the oven and transfer to a container. Cover with plastic wrap and allow to cool.

Remove the blackened skin from the capsicums by gently rubbing it away with your fingers. The skin should come away easily. Remove the stems and the seeds from inside the capsicum. Lay the cleaned flesh on a board and finely slice or chop it.

Season and toss with a little olive oil before serving with barbecued tuna, swordfish or spiced chicken. Mix with some pitted olives and serve with roast beef or grilled lamb. If not using straight away then marinate the red capsicum in olive oil with garlic and basil leaves.

sautéed mushrooms

400 g (14 oz) Swiss brown mushrooms
40 g (1½ oz) butter
1 garlic clove, finely chopped

Put the mushrooms in a pan with the butter, garlic and a little sea salt. Heat over medium heat and when the butter begins to sizzle, cover with a lid and reduce the heat to low. Cook for 10 minutes, then remove from the heat. Season with freshly ground black pepper before serving.

Serve with scrambled eggs and crispy bacon or as an accompaniment to grilled steak.

tapenade

makes 250 ml (9 fl oz/1 cup)

80 g (2³/₄ oz/¹/₂ cup) pitted kalamata
  olives
1 garlic clove
1 handful roughly chopped flat-leaf
  (Italian) parsley
10 basil leaves
2 anchovy fillets
1 teaspoon capers, rinsed and drained
3 tablespoons olive oil

Put the olives, garlic, parsley, basil, anchovies and capers into a blender or food processor and blend to a rough paste. Add the olive oil in a stream until you reach the desired consistency. Season with freshly ground black pepper to taste.

Serve as a dollop on barbecued tuna or lamb fillets or spread on crusty white bread and serve with sliced tomatoes and salami.

oven-roasted tomatoes

serves 2

2 roma (plum) tomatoes
a few thyme sprigs
extra virgin olive oil, to drizzle

Preheat the oven to 180°C (350°F/ Gas 4). Slice the tomatoes in half lengthways and put in a roasting tin lined with baking paper. Scatter with the thyme sprigs and season liberally with sea salt and freshly ground black pepper. Drizzle with a little extra virgin olive oil and bake for 40 minutes.

Serve with creamy scrambled eggs, grilled sausages or barbecued tuna.

artichoke, oregano and prosciutto pizza capsicum salad
red onion tart warm salad of fennel and salami
cumin tortillas with roasted capsicums romano pizza
warm leek salad fresh tomato and oregano salad pan
bagna pine mushroom salad margherita pizza white
bean salad roast capsicum and green olive salad
chilli corn cakes pissaladière sardines on toast
summer salad with spiced goat's curd tapenade

02 light meals

black bean salsa with tortilla grilled polenta with
mushrooms jewelled gazpacho prosciutto and sugar
snap salad niçoise salad roast pumpkin salad
capriciosa pizza marinated seared prawns with
bruschetta mushrooms baked in vine leaves three bean

artichoke, oregano and prosciutto pizza

makes 4

2 vine-ripened tomatoes
4 tablespoons olive oil
1 quantity pizza dough (basics)
8 slices prosciutto, cut in half
175 g (6 oz) jar marinated artichoke
    hearts, drained and sliced
100 g (3 1/2 oz) goat's cheese
a few oregano leaves, to garnish

Preheat the oven to 200°C (400°F/ Gas 6). Cut the tomatoes into eighths and put them onto a baking tray. Season with a little sea salt and drizzle with 2 tablespoons of olive oil. Roast the tomatoes for 15 minutes. Remove from the oven.

Roll out four small rounds of the pizza dough, each one about 12 cm (4 1/2 in) in diameter. Put onto a baking tray and top with the prosciutto, roasted tomatoes, artichoke hearts and goat's cheese. Drizzle with a little olive oil and season with sea salt. Bake for 15 minutes, then garnish with a few oregano leaves.

red capsicum salad

serves 4

2 red capsicums (peppers)
2 garlic cloves, thinly sliced
4 anchovies, finely chopped
4 small ripe roma (plum) tomatoes,
  halved
4 tablespoons olive oil
1 handful flat-leaf (Italian) parsley
2 witlof (chicory/Belgian endive),
  washed and thinly sliced
2 boiled eggs, finely chopped
1 tablespoon salted capers, rinsed
  and drained

Preheat the oven to 200°C (400°F/ Gas 6). Cut the capsicums in half and remove any seeds. Put the capsicum halves, open side up, on a baking tray. Scatter with the garlic and anchovies. Place a tomato half inside each capsicum half. Drizzle with the olive oil and season with sea salt and freshly ground black pepper. Bake for 1 hour.

Divide the parsley and witlof among four plates. Put a capsicum half on each plate. Scatter with the chopped egg and capers. Drizzle with the pan juices and serve immediately.

red onion tart

1¹/2 sheets butter puff pastry
30 g (1 oz) butter
1 large pinch saffron threads
1 kg (2 lb 4 oz) red onions, thinly sliced
125 ml (4 fl oz/¹/2 cup) white wine
1 heaped teaspoon sea salt
1 teaspoon cracked black pepper
4 egg yolks
250 ml (9 fl oz/1 cup) thick
   (double/heavy) cream
50 g (1³/4 oz/¹/2 cup) grated parmesan
   cheese

Preheat the oven to 180°C (350°F/ Gas 4). Line a 25 cm (10 in) flan tin with the pastry and chill until needed. Heat the butter and saffron in a large frying pan over medium heat. Add the onions and cook, stirring often, until they are soft and transparent. Pour in the white wine, cover the pan and simmer on low heat for a further 40 minutes, or until the onions are buttery soft and slightly caramelized.

Prick the pastry base with a fork and bake it blind for 15 minutes. Remove the baking weights and bake for a further 5–10 minutes, or until the base is golden.

When the onions are cooked, add the salt and pepper and tip them into the tart case. Whisk the yolks and cream together and pour over the onions. Sprinkle on the parmesan and bake for 30 minutes, or until the filling has set and is golden brown. Serve with a salad of bitter leaves.

warm salad of fennel and salami

serves 4

340 g (11¾ oz) small fennel bulbs
10 sprigs thyme
4 tablespoons extra virgin olive oil
2 tablespoons balsamic vinegar
16 slices spicy salami
120 g (4¼ oz) rocket (arugula)
150 g (5½ oz/1 cup) crumbled creamy
  Persian feta cheese

Preheat the oven to 180°C (350°F/ Gas 4). Slice the fennel bulbs lengthways into quarters or eighths, depending on how big they are and put them on a baking tray. Add the thyme and olive oil. Toss everything together, season and then cover with foil and bake for 30 minutes.

When the fennel has cooked through, drizzle it with the balsamic vinegar. Lay the salami slices on a baking tray and put them under the grill (broiler) for 2–3 minutes, or until slightly crisp. Arrange the rocket on four plates and top with the fennel, salami and feta.

cumin tortillas with roasted capsicums

makes 12

tortillas

310 g (11 oz/2½ cups) plain (all-purpose) flour
½ teaspoon baking powder
2 teaspoons ground cumin
100 ml (3½ fl oz) canola oil
1 tablespoon lime juice
170 g (6 oz/⅔ cup) plain yoghurt

roasted capsicum filling

2 roasted red capsicums (peppers), skinned and seeds removed, sliced into thin strips
10 basil leaves, torn
1 tablespoon balsamic vinegar
350 g (12 oz) tuna fillet, sliced into three lengthways

Sift the flour, baking powder and cumin into a large bowl. Add the oil and mix well to form a dough. In a bowl, combine the lime juice, yoghurt and ½ teaspoon of salt. Drizzle over the flour and slowly combine until the dough begins to soften. Gather into a ball and lightly knead until smooth. Divide into 12 portions. Taking one portion at a time, roll out on a floured surface to form a very thin 18 cm (7 in) circle. Set aside and repeat with the remaining portions, placing baking paper or plastic wrap between each tortilla.

Heat a large frying pan over medium heat. Cook the tortillas, turning once, so that each side is golden brown. Remove and keep warm by covering with a tea towel. Toss the capsicum together with the basil, vinegar and 1 teaspoon of salt. Quickly sear the tuna fillets on all sides. Thinly slice and place on the tortillas. Top with some of the roasted capsicum filling, roll up and serve.

romano pizza

500 g (1 lb 2 oz) bocconcini (fresh baby
  mozzarella cheese)
2 medium pizza bases (basics)
6 anchovies, roughly chopped
extra virgin olive oil, to drizzle
basil leaves, to serve

Preheat the oven to 200°C (400°F/ Gas 6). Spread half of the cheese over the 2 pizza bases. Scatter half of the anchovies over the bases. Bake for 15 minutes. Remove from the oven and top with the remaining cheese and anchovies. Drizzle with extra virgin olive oil, season with a little sea salt and return to the oven. Bake until the cheese has just melted. Scatter over the basil leaves before serving.

warm leek salad   serves 4

1 generous pinch saffron
60 g (2¼ oz) butter
125 ml (4 fl oz/½ cup) white wine
24 baby leeks
4 slices prosciutto
1 tablespoon olive oil
12 sage leaves
16 niçoise olives
70 g (2½ oz) creamy blue cheese
1 tablespoon small capers, rinsed
   and drained

Preheat the oven to 180°C (350°F/ Gas 4). Put a deep roasting tin over high heat and sprinkle in the saffron, letting it heat through before adding the butter. As it sizzles, add the wine and leeks. Remove the tin from the heat, cover with foil and bake for 40 minutes. Meanwhile, heat a frying pan and cook the prosciutto until it is crisp and golden. Drain on paper towels. Add the olive oil to the pan and fry the sage leaves. When they begin to crisp up, remove and drain on paper towels. Toss the olives in the hot oil and then remove the pan from the heat, leaving the olives in the pan.

When the leeks are cooked, arrange on four warmed plates. Top with the prosciutto, cheese, capers, sage leaves and olives. Pour over some of the juices from the frying pan and the roasting tin.

fresh tomato and oregano salad

serves 4

1 small onion, halved and thinly sliced
2 teaspoons white sugar
1 tablespoon white wine vinegar
2 vine-ripened tomatoes
170 g (6 oz) oregano, leaves only
extra virgin olive oil, to drizzle

Toss the onion and sugar together and allow to stand for 30 minutes before adding the vinegar. Cut the tomatoes into eighths and sprinkle them with sea salt and freshly ground black pepper.

Just before serving the salad, toss the tomatoes, onion and oregano leaves together and add a trickle of extra virgin olive oil.

pan bagna

1 thin baguette
1 tablespoon virgin olive oil
1 garlic clove, peeled and sliced in half
2 red capsicums (peppers), roasted,
  skin and seeds removed
1 tablespoon salted capers, rinsed
  and drained
185 g (6¹/2 oz) tin tuna, drained
15 black olives, pitted
1/2 small red onion, thinly sliced
15 basil leaves
1 large handful roughly chopped
  flat-leaf (Italian) parsley
10 anchovies
100 g (3¹/2 oz) marinated artichoke
  hearts, drained, sliced

With a sharp bread knife, slice the baguette in half down its length and remove the bread filling from both the top and bottom portions. Brush the interior of the loaf with olive oil and rub with garlic.

Cut the roasted capsicum into thin strips and combine with the remaining ingredients in a bowl. Season with salt and freshly ground black pepper and spoon inside the bottom half of the loaf, heaping it up. Reassemble the loaf, making sure that the sides meet neatly. Wrap in plastic wrap, put a weight on top (a breadboard or heavy saucepan is suitable) and put in the refrigerator overnight. Slice into 2 cm (3/4 in) widths and serve.

salad of sweet onions and prosciutto

serves 4

2 tablespoons olive oil

8 slices prosciutto, halved

12 spring onions (scallions), trimmed and halved

20 g (3/4 oz) thyme

1 tablespoon soft brown sugar

2 tablespoons balsamic vinegar

125 ml (4 fl oz/1/2 cup) red wine

2 ripe tomatoes, finely diced

1 radicchio, trimmed, leaves washed

4 slices rye bread, toasted

2 tablespoons extra virgin olive oil

Heat the olive oil in a large frying pan over medium heat and fry the prosciutto until lightly crisp. Drain on paper towels. Add the spring onions to the pan with the thyme sprigs. Reduce the heat to low, sprinkle with the sugar and add the vinegar and wine. Cover and cook slowly for 10 minutes.

Put the tomatoes in a bowl. Season with sea salt and freshly ground black pepper. Put the radicchio over the spring onions for a few minutes, or until it begins to wilt. Toss the spring onions and tomatoes together.

To assemble, put the rye toast on four plates. Top with the radicchio, spoon over the tomato and spring onions then top with the prosciutto. Drizzle with extra virgin olive oil and serve immediately.

margherita pizza

serves 4

400 g (14 oz) tin roma (plum) tomatoes
2 tablespoons extra virgin olive oil
2 medium pizza bases (basics)
extra virgin olive oil, extra, to drizzle
250 g (9 oz) bocconcini (fresh
   baby mozzarella cheese), sliced
2 tablespoons grated parmesan
   cheese
oregano leaves, to serve

Preheat the oven to 200°C (400°F/ Gas 6). Drain and finely chop the tomatoes. Put the tomatoes in a saucepan with the oil and simmer over medium heat for 5 minutes, or until the tomatoes are no longer watery. Allow to cool. Spread the tomato evenly over the pizza bases. Season with a little sea salt, drizzle with a little of the oil and bake for 15 minutes. Remove from the oven and top with the bocconcini and parmesan. Return to the oven for a few minutes until the cheese has melted. Top with the oregano leaves.

pine mushroom salad   serves 4

2 garlic bulbs
3 tablespoons extra virgin olive oil
1 tablespoon balsamic vinegar
white pepper, to season
a pinch sugar
4 large pine mushrooms
2 tablespoons light olive oil
40 g (1½ oz/¼ cup) pine nuts, toasted
150 g (5½ oz) flat-leaf (Italian) parsley,
    roughly chopped
40 g (1½ oz/⅓ cup) shaved parmesan
    cheese
1 sourdough baguette

Preheat the oven to 200°C (400°F/ Gas 6). Wrap the garlic bulbs in foil and bake them in the oven for 30 minutes, or until the cloves are soft and a little mushy. Slice the garlic in half and squeeze the soft cloves into a small bowl. Mash the garlic with a fork, then add the extra virgin olive oil and vinegar. Season with a little salt, white pepper and a pinch of sugar. If the sauce is quite thick, add 2 tablespoons of hot water to thin it down.

Meanwhile, brush the mushrooms with the light olive oil and bake them in the oven for 20 minutes, or until they are just beginning to soften.

Slice half of the mushrooms. Put in a bowl with the pine nuts and parsley and the whole mushrooms. Add the garlic sauce and lightly toss the salad. Top with the parmesan and serve with thinly sliced and toasted sourdough bread.

white bean and tomato salad

serves 4

2 tablespoons olive oil

2 garlic cloves, crushed

1 red onion, cut into wedges

50 g (1¾ oz) thyme, broken into sprigs

3 tablespoons white wine

400 g (14 oz) tin cannellini beans

150 g (5½ oz) cherry tomatoes, halved

1 tablespoon balsamic vinegar

5 handfuls roughly chopped flat-leaf
  (Italian) parsley

virgin olive oil (optional)

Heat the oil in a frying pan over medium heat. Add the garlic. Cook until lightly golden before adding the red onion and thyme. Continue cooking until the onion is soft and transparent, then pour in the white wine. Simmer until the wine has reduced to almost nothing before mixing in the beans. Stir to combine and then remove the bean mixture from the heat.

Tip the beans into a bowl, add the tomatoes, vinegar and parsley, stir to combine and season to taste. You can also add a little virgin olive oil to give the salad a rich gloss.

chicken and pine nut salad

1 egg yolk
1 teaspoon balsamic vinegar
125 ml (4 fl oz/1/2 cup) light olive oil
2 anchovies, finely chopped
2 chicken breasts (400 g/14 oz),
  poached and shredded
40 g (11/2 oz/1/4 cup) salted capers,
  rinsed and drained
40 g (11/2 oz/1/4 cup) pine nuts, toasted
35 g (11/4 oz/1/4 cup) currants
1 large handful roughly chopped
  flat-leaf (Italian) parsley
zest of 1 lemon

Place the egg yolk and vinegar in a small bowl and whisk to combine. Slowly add the oil, whisking to form a thick, creamy mayonnaise. Fold the anchovies through the mayonnaise and season with salt and freshly ground black pepper. Set aside.

Place the remaining ingredients in a large bowl and toss together. Fold in the anchovy mayonnaise. Serve the salad in small bowls and season with cracked black pepper to taste.

mushrooms baked in vine leaves

serves 4

24 vine leaves in brine
4 large field mushrooms, stalks
    removed
12 cherry tomatoes
2 red onions, cut into eight wedges
4 sprigs thyme
4 tablespoons extra virgin olive oil
crusty bread, to serve
goat's cheese, to serve
fresh pesto (basics), to serve

Preheat the oven to 180°C (350°F/ Gas 4). Rinse the vine leaves. Drain in a colander. Lay out four pieces of baking paper, each approximately 20 cm (8 in) square. Lay three large vine leaves at the centre of every square, overlapping the leaves to make a base. Sit one of the field mushrooms in the middle of each, cap side down.

Divide the cherry tomatoes, onions and thyme between the four mushrooms, piling them up in the cap. Pour over the olive oil and cover the mushrooms with another three vine leaves, tucking the edges under to make a parcel. Draw in the four corners of each baking paper square so that they meet, then twist the joined corners to fasten the edges and seal. Put the parcels onto a baking tray and bake for 1 1/2 hours.

To serve, remove the baking paper and the top leaves, so the vegetables are sitting on a bed of baked vine leaves. Serve with crusty bread, goat's cheese and pesto.

capriciosa pizza

400 g (14 oz) tin roma (plum) tomatoes
2 tablespoons extra virgin olive oil
2 medium pizza bases (basics)
extra virgin olive oil, to drizzle
250 g (9 oz) sliced bocconcini (fresh baby mozzarella cheese)
100 g (3½ oz) sliced ham
50 g (1¾ oz/½ cup) button mushrooms, sliced
110 g (3¾ oz/½ cup) sliced marinated artichoke hearts
80 g (2¾ oz/½ cup) pitted kalamata olives
2 tablespoons grated parmesan cheese

Preheat the oven to 200°C (400°F/ Gas 6). Drain and thinly slice the tomatoes. Put the tomatoes in a saucepan with the oil. Simmer over medium heat for 5 minutes. Allow to cool. Spread the tomato over the pizza bases. Season with sea salt, drizzle with a little extra virgin olive oil and bake for 15 minutes. Remove from the oven and top with the bocconcini, ham, mushrooms, artichoke hearts and olives. Sprinkle with parmesan and return to the oven for a few minutes until the cheese has melted.

fennel and tomato salad

serves 4

3 fennel bulbs, trimmed
1 tablespoon thyme leaves
2 tablespoons lemon juice
160 ml (5¼ fl oz) extra virgin olive oil
500 g (1 lb 2 oz) truss tomatoes,
    stalks intact
1 tablespoon balsamic vinegar
1 teaspoon caster (superfine) sugar
70 g (2½ oz/¾ cup) shaved parmesan
    cheese
1 handful basil leaves
crusty bread, to serve

Preheat the oven to 200°C (400°F/ Gas 6). Cut the fennel bulbs from top to base into several thick slices. Place on a baking tray with the thyme, drizzle with the lemon juice and 4 tablespoons of the oil. Cover with foil and put in the oven.

Place the tomatoes on a smaller baking tray and drizzle with the vinegar and remaining olive oil. Sprinkle with the sugar, cover with foil and put in the oven. Bake the tomatoes and fennel for 30 minutes, or until the tomatoes are beginning to burst.

To assemble, layer the tomatoes, fennel and parmesan with the basil leaves. Spoon over the cooking liquids and serve with crusty bread.

warm roast beef salad

4 roma (plum) tomatoes, quartered
   lengthways
pinch white sugar
125 ml (4 fl oz/1/2 cup) oil
1 large eggplant (aubergine),
   thinly sliced
450 g (1 lb) piece beef fillet
240 g (81/2 oz) rocket (arugula)
90 g (3/4 oz/1/3 cup) fresh pesto (basics)

Preheat the oven to 180°C (350°F/ Gas 4). Put the tomatoes on a baking tray and season them with salt, pepper and a little white sugar. Put them in the oven for about 20 minutes. Heat the oil in a frying pan over high heat and fry the eggplant slices until they are lightly browned on both sides. Remove the eggplant and drain on paper towels. Pour away most of the oil and return the pan to high heat.

Sear the beef fillet in the frying pan. Put on a baking tray and in the oven for 10 minutes (it will be rare at this point, so cook it for another 5 minutes if you prefer). Season the beef with salt, cover with foil and allow to rest for a few minutes.

Arrange the tomatoes and eggplant on a bed of rocket leaves. Thinly slice the beef, arrange on the salad and season well. Finish with a spoonful of pesto on top of the beef.

provençal tart

4 large red onions, cut into six wedges
2 tablespoons olive oil
a few thyme sprigs
1 tablespoon balsamic vinegar
1 pre-baked 25 cm (10 in) shortcrust
  tart case (basics)
3 ripe Roma (plum) tomatoes,
  thickly sliced
10 kalamata olives, pitted and torn
extra virgin olive oil, to drizzle
torn basil leaves
green salad or goat's cheese, to serve

Preheat the oven to 180°C (350°F/ Gas 4). Put the onions in a heavy-based frying pan with the oil and thyme. Sauté over low heat for 20 minutes, or until the onion is beginning to soften and lightly caramelize. Add the balsamic vinegar, stir to combine and cook for a further 5 minutes. Remove from the heat.

Spread the onion in the tart case. Arrange the tomato slices over the onion. Scatter the olives over the sliced tomato. Season with salt and freshly ground black pepper. Cover with foil and bake for 20 minutes. Remove the foil and bake for a further 15 minutes. Remove from the oven, drizzle with a little extra virgin olive oil and add a scattering of torn basil leaves. Serve with a green salad or goat's cheese.

roast pumpkin salad   serves 4

2 red capsicums (peppers), roasted
800 g (1 lb 12 oz) pumpkin (winter
    squash), peeled
4 tablespoons olive oil
1 tablespoon finely chopped
    lemon grass
1 tablespoon lemon juice
1 teaspoon sesame oil
1 teaspoon shaved palm sugar
1 teaspoon soy sauce
100 g (3 1/2 oz/2 cups) baby rocket
    (arugula) leaves

Preheat the oven to 180°C (350°F/ Gas 4). Roast the capsicums until the skin is blistered or blackened. Put into a bowl, cover with plastic wrap and set aside.

Chop the pumpkin into eight large pieces. Put on a baking tray. Rub with half the oil and place in the oven. Bake for 40 minutes, or until the pumpkin is cooked through.

Meanwhile, peel and seed the capsicums. Finely dice the flesh. Put in a bowl with the lemon grass, lemon juice, sesame oil, palm sugar, soy sauce and remaining olive oil. Stir to combine.

Serve the baked pumpkin on a bed of rocket leaves. Spoon over the capsicum mixture. Season with freshly ground black pepper.

roast capsicum and green olive salad

serves 6

2 red capsicums (peppers)
2 green capsicums (peppers)
2 yellow capsicums (peppers)
2 garlic cloves, finely chopped
75 g (2^{1}/$_{2}$ oz) parsley, roughly chopped
10 large basil leaves, roughly chopped
12 green olives, pitted and sliced
3 tablespoons olive oil
1 tablespoon balsamic vinegar

Roast the capsicums whole in a 200°C (400°F/Gas 6) oven until the skin blisters, then put them in a plastic bag or covered bowl and allow to cool. Seed and skin the capsicums, then thinly slice them and put them in a bowl with the garlic, parsley, basil, sliced green olives, olive oil and balsamic vinegar.

Toss the ingredients to combine. Season with sea salt and freshly ground black pepper.

pissaladière

4 tablespoons olive oil
4–5 large onions, thinly sliced
1 teaspoon finely chopped rosemary
1 teaspoon finely chopped thyme
1 teaspoon caster (superfine) sugar
1 quantity risen pizza dough (basics)
12 anchovies
16 black olives, pitted
12 basil leaves, to garnish

Preheat the oven 220°C (425°F/ Gas 7). Heat a large frying pan over medium heat and add the olive oil, onions, rosemary and thyme. Cover and cook over a low heat for 20 minutes, or until the onions are very soft. Add the sugar and cook for a further minute before setting aside. Turn out the risen dough onto a floured surface and punch it down. Divide into four sections and roll out each piece to form a thin oval. Turn the edges over a little to form a slightly thicker crust. Put on a large oiled baking tray. Cover the surface of the pizzas with the onions. Tear the anchovies and olives into small pieces and dot over the onions. Bake for 15 minutes. Remove from the oven and garnish with torn basil leaves.

three bean salad with prosciutto

serves 4

6 slices prosciutto
175 g (6 oz) green beans
175 g (6 oz) wax beans
175 g (6 oz) tinned butterbeans
  (lima beans), rinsed and drained
2 tablespoons extra virgin olive oil
2 tablespoons white wine vinegar
5 handfuls flat-leaf (Italian) parsley,
  roughly chopped
2 tablespoons pine nuts, toasted

Bring a large saucepan of water to the boil. Meanwhile, grill (broil) or pan-fry the prosciutto until it is crisp and then allow to drain on a paper towel.

Blanch the green and wax beans in the boiling water for a few minutes. or until the green ones begin to turn an emerald green. Drain the beans and refresh under cold running water.

Return the beans to the saucepan with the butter beans and add the olive oil, vinegar and parsley. Break the prosciutto into small pieces and add to the beans along with the pine nuts. Toss together and season with sea salt and black pepper. Pile onto a serving platter.

sardines on toast

3 ripe tomatoes, finely diced
1/2 red onion, thinly sliced into rings
2 tablespoons white wine vinegar
2 tablespoons virgin olive oil
1 tablespoon oregano leaves
5 g (1/4 oz) butter
8 or 16 sardine fillets depending on
     their size (300 g/10 1/2 oz in total)
4 thick slices wholemeal (whole-wheat)
     bread, toasted

Put the tomatoes, onion, vinegar, olive oil and oregano leaves in a bowl. Stir to combine and season with sea salt and freshly ground black pepper. Heat a non-stick frying pan over high heat and add the butter. Fry the sardine fillets for 1–2 minutes on both sides, or until they are opaque and slightly browned. Pile the sardines onto the toast. Top with the tomato salad and any remaining dressing.

black bean salsa with tortilla

serves 4

2 tablespoons olive oil

1 garlic clove, crushed

1 tablespoon ground cumin

1 red capsicum (pepper), finely diced

200 g (7 oz/1 cup) fresh corn kernels

220 g (7³/₄ oz/1 cup) cooked black turtle beans

2 large handfuls coriander (cilantro), roughly chopped

1 large handful mint leaves, roughly chopped

1 tablespoon pomegranate molasses

finely chopped chipotle chilli or Tabasco sauce

rocket (arugula), sour cream and tortillas, to serve

Heat the olive oil in a frying pan over medium heat and add the garlic, ground cumin and diced capsicum. Sauté until the capsicum is soft and then add the corn and black turtle beans. Cook for a further 5 minutes, or until the corn is golden and soft. Remove the corn and bean mixture from the heat and put into a serving bowl. Add the herbs and pomegranate molasses and season to taste with salt, pepper and the chipotle chilli or Tabasco sauce. Serve with rocket, sour cream and warm tortillas, or as a side dish to spicy grilled chicken.

marinated seared prawns
with bruschetta
serves 4

4 garlic cloves

1 tablespoon grated fresh ginger

1 large red chilli, seeded

1/2 teaspoon ground white pepper

1 tablespoon sesame oil

125 ml (4 fl oz/1/2 cup) olive oil

1 lemon, juiced

16 large raw prawns (shrimps), peeled
and deveined with tails intact

4 thin slices sourdough bread, cut on
the diagonal

50 g (13/4 oz) baby English spinach
leaves

2 spring onions (scallions), thinly sliced

Put the garlic, ginger, chilli, white pepper, sesame oil, olive oil and lemon juice into a food processor and blend until combined. Put the prawns in a bowl, add the marinade and toss until they are well covered. Cover and place in the fridge for 1 hour.

Toast the sourdough and put on separate serving plates. Pile with the spinach and spring onions.

Sear the prawns in a frying pan over high heat for 2–3 minutes, or until they are pink and starting to curl. Divide the prawns among the four plates. Pour the remaining marinade into the pan and warm over medium heat. Spoon the hot garlicky oil over the prawns and serve immediately.

chilli corn cakes   serves 4 to 6

420 g (15 oz) tin creamed corn
125 g (4¹/₂ oz/1 cup) fine semolina
125 g (4¹/₂ oz) mozzarella cheese, grated
125 g (4¹/₂ oz) goat's cheese, crumbled
4 tablespoons finely chopped coriander (cilantro)
1 teaspoon baking powder
3 jalapeño chillies, finely chopped
2 eggs
125 ml (4 fl oz/¹/₂ cup) vegetable oil
6 slices bacon
4 handfuls baby English spinach leaves

Mix the creamed corn, semolina, mozzarella, goat's cheese, coriander, baking powder, chillies and eggs together. Season with sea salt and freshly ground black pepper.

Heat a lightly oiled non-stick frying pan over medium heat and cook the bacon until crispy. Remove and keep warm until ready to serve. Add 2 tablespoons of vegetable oil to the pan. Add 2 heaped tablespoons of the batter to form a round corn cake and cook for 3 minutes on each side, or until golden and crusty. Remove and continue with the remaining batter, adding more oil when needed. Serve warm with the bacon and baby English spinach leaves.

summer salad with spiced goat's curd

100 g (3¹/₂ oz) goat's curd or light
  goat's cheese
1 teaspoon ground cumin
milk (optional)
100 g (3¹/₂ oz) green beans, trimmed
4 roma (plum) tomatoes
2 Lebanese (short) cucumbers
10 mint leaves
2 spring onions (scallions), thinly sliced
1 handful flat-leaf (Italian) parsley
4 tablespoons extra virgin olive oil
1 tablespoon lemon juice

Put the goat's curd into a bowl with the cumin and a grind of black pepper. Stir together to form a soft, thick cream. Add a little milk to the mixture, if needed, to make it softer and easier to stir.

Blanch the green beans in boiling salted water. When they turn bright green, drain and rinse under running cold water. Cut the beans into thin diagonal strips and put in a large bowl. Thickly dice the tomatoes and cucumbers and add them to the beans. Season with sea salt, then add the mint, spring onions, parsley, extra virgin olive oil and lemon juice. Toss together and divide among four plates. Top with a spoonful of the goat's curd.

grilled polenta with mushrooms

5 g (1/8 oz) dried porcini mushrooms
20 g (3/4 oz) butter
1 garlic clove, finely chopped
100 g (31/2 oz) Swiss brown mushrooms, thinly sliced
100 g (31/2 oz) fresh shiitake mushrooms, thinly sliced
100 g (31/2 oz) oyster mushrooms
1 quantity polenta (basics)
150 g (51/2 oz) rocket (arugula), stalks removed
2 tablespoons extra virgin olive oil

Put the porcini mushrooms in a bowl. Cover with 250 ml (9 fl oz/1 cup) warm water. Squeeze any excess liquid from the porcini mushrooms, reserving their soaking liquid, and thinly slice. Put into a deep frying pan with the butter and garlic. Cook over low heat until the garlic is golden. Add the reserved soaking liquid from the porcini, then the Swiss brown and shiitake mushrooms. Cover with a lid and simmer for 10 minutes. If the mixture becomes a little dry, add some more water to give the mushrooms a wet texture. At the end of cooking time, add the whole oyster mushrooms. Cook for a further 3 minutes. Season with sea salt and freshly cracked black pepper.

With a sharp knife, mark out the polenta into large triangles. Cook the polenta under a grill (broiler) until the top is golden brown. Pile the warm polenta triangles onto a bed of rocket leaves on four warmed plates. Top with the mushrooms. Drizzle with a little extra virgin olive oil.

jewelled gazpacho

4 Lebanese (short) cucumbers
8 ripe tomatoes, roughly chopped
1 tablespoon sea salt
1 teaspoon ground roast cumin seeds
1 small beetroot, peeled and chopped
1 red capsicum (pepper), diced
3 spring onions (scallions), thinly sliced
1/2 red onion, finely diced
2 tablespoons chopped coriander
  (cilantro) leaves
extra virgin olive oil, to drizzle

Roughly chop 2 of the cucumbers and finely dice the remaining 2. Put the tomatoes and chopped cucumber into a large bowl with the sea salt and the ground cumin seeds. Stir well and leave to marinate for 2 hours. Put the tomato and cucumber mixture into a blender or food processor with the beetroot and whiz to a purée.

Pour the purée into a muslin-lined strainer over a bowl, twist the muslin into a ball and squeeze out all the liquid. Discard the pulp and chill the juice. When the juice is cold, add the capsicum, spring onions, onion and coriander and chill the gazpacho for a further 1 hour. Season to taste, ladle into individual bowls and serve with a drizzle of extra virgin olive oil.

prosciutto and sugar snap salad

serves 4

3 tablespoons olive oil
8 slices prosciutto
2 fennel bulbs, finely shaved
200 g (7 oz) sugar snap peas, blanched
   and sliced on the diagonal
10 mint leaves, torn
1 lemon, juiced

Heat the olive oil in a large frying pan over medium heat and fry the prosciutto until just crisp. Set aside to drain on paper towels. Put the fennel, peas and mint into a bowl. Drizzle with the oil from the pan and the lemon juice. Break the crisp prosciutto into small pieces ad add to the salad. Toss together and divide among four plates.

tapenade linguine   serves 4

5 handfuls roughly chopped flat-leaf
  (Italian) parsley
45 g (1¹/2 oz/¹/4 cup) pitted and
  chopped black olives
1 lemon, zested
4–6 anchovies, finely chopped
1 tablespoon salted capers, rinsed
  and drained
70 g (2¹/2 oz/1³/4 cup) shaved
  parmesan cheese
3 tablespoons extra virgin olive oil
400 g (14 oz) linguine

To make the tapenade, put the parsley, olives, lemon zest, anchovies, capers, parmesan and olive oil into a large bowl and toss them together.

Cook the pasta in boiling water until *al dente*, then drain and return to the saucepan. Add the tapenade, toss it through the linguine and divide among four pasta bowls.

niçoise salad

8 small potatoes
150 g (5¹/2 oz) green beans
4 eggs
2 small butter lettuces
175 g (6 oz) tin Italian-style tuna,
   drained
2 ripe tomatoes, cut into chunks
1/2 red onion, thinly sliced
20 kalamata olives
1 handful flat-leaf (Italian) parsley
20 g (³/4 oz) salted capers, rinsed
   and drained
8 anchovies

dressing
2 tablespoons lemon juice
4 tablespoons extra virgin olive oil
1/4 teaspoon crushed garlic

Boil the potatoes until cooked through, then drain and cut in half. Blanch the green beans in boiling water until emerald green, then drain and rinse. Boil the eggs for 6 minutes.

Divide the leaves from the butter lettuces among four bowls. Shell the eggs and cut in half. Divide the potatoes, beans and eggs among the bowls. Add the tuna to the bowls along with the tomatoes and red onion. Add the olives to each bowl with a light scattering of parsley and salted capers.

To make the dressing, combine the lemon juice, olive oil and garlic. Drizzle the dressing over the salads and then top each salad with the anchovies.

fresh fig and prosciutto pizza

1 quantity pizza dough (basics)
120 g (4¹/4 oz) taleggio cheese,
    thinly sliced
4 fresh figs, thinly sliced
4 slices prosciutto, halved
olive oil, to drizzle
1 handful baby rocket (arugula) leaves,
    to serve

Preheat the oven to 200°C (400°F/ Gas 6). Roll out four small circles of the pizza dough, each one about 12 cm (4¹/2 in) in diameter. Put onto a baking tray and top with the sliced taleggio, figs and prosciutto. Drizzle with a little olive oil and season with salt and freshly ground black pepper. Bake for 15 minutes, or until the dough is golden brown. Serve with a scattering of rocket leaves.

roasted red capsicum soup with minted yoghurt seared tuna with olive butter and warm red salad chilli corn and black bean soup warm vegetables with white beans fresh lasagne with chilli crab chilli mussels fish, clam and herb soup lamb shanks with parsnip lemon and herbs swordfish with prosciutto osso bucco seaside risoni linguine with prawns and fresh herbs vine leaf chicken lamb cutlets with mint salsa roast

03   mains

tuna with fennel and tomato snapper sausage and bean stew tomato risotto salsa mussels with rouille risoni with sweet and sour capsicum pancetta and pea risotto tuna with tomato and olives steak with onion salsa blue eye cod with saffron and capers parmesan

roasted red capsicum soup
with minted yoghurt   serves 4

4 red capsicums (peppers)
4 vine-ripened tomatoes, stems
   removed
1 tablespoon olive oil
750 ml (26 fl oz/3 cups) vegetable
   stock (basics)
1 teaspoon finely chopped tinned
   chipotle chilli
1 teaspoon ground cumin
90 g (3 1/4 oz/1/3 cup) plain yoghurt
1 tablespoon finely chopped mint

Preheat the oven to 200°C (400°F/ Gas 6). Put the capsicums and tomatoes onto a baking tray and rub with the olive oil. Bake in the oven for 30 minutes, or until both the capsicums and tomatoes are slightly blackened and blistered. Remove and allow to cool. Remove the skins and seeds from the capsicums and then put into a food processor with the tomatoes. Process into a smooth purée and put in a saucepan with the stock, chilli and cumin. Bring to the boil and then reduce the heat to low. Simmer the soup for 10 minutes and season to taste with sea salt and freshly ground black pepper.

In a small bowl, combine the yoghurt and mint. Ladle the soup into warmed bowls and add a spoonful of the minted yoghurt.

pancetta and pea risotto

1 litre (35 fl oz/4 cups) chicken stock (basics)
40 g (1¹/2 oz) butter
1 onion, finely diced
8 slices pancetta, finely chopped
4 sage leaves, thinly sliced
225 g (8 oz/1 cup) risotto rice
150 g (5¹/2 oz/1 cup) frozen peas
70 g (2¹/2 oz/³/4 cup) grated parmesan cheese
1 small handful flat-leaf (Italian) parsley
olive oil, to drizzle

Boil the chicken stock in a saucepan. Heat the butter in a large heavy-based saucepan over medium heat and add the onion, pancetta and sage. Sauté until the onion is soft and transparent. Add the risotto rice. Stir for 1 minute, or until the grains are well coated and glossy. Add 250 ml (9 fl oz/1 cup) of stock, simmer and stir until absorbed. Add another 250 ml (9 fl oz/1 cup) of stock and stir until absorbed. Add the frozen peas and 250 ml (9 fl oz/1 cup) of stock, stirring until absorbed. Test if the rice is *al dente*. If not fully cooked, add the remaining stock and simmer until the stock has reduced and the rice is coated in a creamy sauce.

Fold the cheese and parsley through the risotto. Spoon into warmed bowls. Serve with a drizzle of olive oil.

seared tuna with olive butter and warm red salad

serves 4

1 red capsicum (pepper)
4 ripe tomatoes, quartered
1 red onion, cut into eight wedges
2 tablespoons extra virgin olive oil
40 g (1½ oz) butter, softened
6 black olives, pitted and finely
  chopped
2 tablespoons finely chopped flat-leaf
  (Italian) parsley
4 x 150 g (5½ oz) tuna fillets

Preheat the oven to 180°C (350°F/ Gas 4). Slice the capsicum into thick strips and put on a baking tray. Add the tomatoes and red onion, drizzle with the olive oil and season with sea salt and freshly ground black pepper. Cover the vegetables with foil and bake for 30 minutes.

Combine the butter, chopped olives and parsley.

Sear the tuna fillets in a pan for 2–3 minutes on both sides. Serve with the warm red salad and a dollop of the olive butter.

fresh lasagne with chilli crab

serves 4

4 tablespoons olive oil

2 large red chillies, seeded and
   thinly sliced

1/2 teaspoon smoked paprika

2 garlic cloves, crushed

3 leeks, thinly sliced

400 g (14 oz) tin chopped tomatoes

1 teaspoon caster (superfine) sugar

125 ml (4 fl oz/1/2 cup) white wine

250 g (9 oz) crab meat

8 fresh lasagne sheets

70 g (21/2 oz/11/2 cups) baby English
   spinach leaves

15 g (1/2 oz) chives, cut into 3 cm
   (11/4 in) lengths

Bring a large pot of salted water to the boil. Heat the olive oil in a large pan over a medium heat and add the chillies, paprika and garlic. Cook for 1 minute before adding the leeks. Cover and simmer for 5 minutes, or until the leeks are soft. Add the tomatoes, 185 ml (6 fl oz/3/4 cup) of water, the sugar and wine. Simmer for a further 10 minutes. Season with sea salt and black pepper.

Put the crab meat into a bowl and break up into fine threads with a fork. Add the crab meat to the tomato sauce.

Cook the lasagne in the boiling water until *al dente*. Drain the lasagne and put a sheet on a warmed plate. Spoon a little sauce onto half the sheet, add the spinach, then fold. Repeat with the remaining ingredients. Serve with a sprinkling of chives.

parmesan lamb pies

serves 4

2 tablespoons olive oil
2 onions, peeled and finely diced
2 garlic cloves, chopped
500 g (1 lb 2 oz) minced (ground) lamb
2 celery stalks, finely chopped
40 g (1¹/2 oz/¹/4 cup) grated carrot
1 teaspoon ground cinnamon
400 g (14 oz) tin chopped tomatoes
250 ml (9 fl oz/1 cup) red wine
3 eggs
200 g (7 oz) Greek-style yoghurt
100 g (3¹/2 oz/1 cup) grated parmesan
  cheese

Preheat the oven to 200°C (400°F/ Gas 6). Heat the olive oil in a frying pan over medium heat, then add the onions and garlic. Cook until the onion begins to soften and turn a golden brown. Add the lamb and increase the heat. Brown the lamb and add the celery, carrot, cinnamon, tomatoes and wine. Reduce the heat to medium and simmer until the liquid has reduced. Season to taste with freshly ground black pepper and sea salt. Spoon the mixture into four individual ramekins or a medium baking dish. Put the eggs, yoghurt and half the parmesan into a bowl and whisk to combine. Spoon the mixture over the pies and sprinkle with the remaining parmesan. Bake for 20 minutes, or until the top is golden brown.

chilli, corn and black bean soup

6 corn cobs
1 tablespoon olive oil
2 red onions, diced
2 garlic cloves, very finely chopped
1 red chilli, seeded and finely chopped
2 tablespoons tomato paste
   (concentrated purée)
1 teaspoon smoked paprika
1 litre (35 fl oz/4 cups) chicken or
   vegetable stock (basics)
200 g (7 oz/1 cup) cooked black beans
90 g (3¼ oz/⅓ cup) sour cream
extra paprika and coriander (cilantro)
   leaves, to serve

With a sharp knife, slice away the kernels from the corn cobs and set aside.

Put a large saucepan over medium heat and add the olive oil, diced onion, garlic and chilli. Cook for 5 minutes, or until the onion is soft and transparent. Add the corn kernels, tomato paste, paprika and stock. Bring to the boil. Reduce the heat to a simmer and cook for 15 minutes. Add the cooked black beans just before serving, then garnish the soup with sour cream, extra paprika and coriander.

pappardelle with basil, feta and roasted capsicum serves 4

4 red capsicums (peppers)
3 tablespoons extra virgin olive oil
1 teaspoon balsamic vinegar
120 g (4¼ oz) basil
400 g (14 oz) pappardelle
150 g (5½ oz) feta cheese

Preheat the oven to 200°C (400°F/ Gas 6). Rub the capsicums with 2 tablespoons of the oil, slice them in half lengthways and put them on a baking tray with the skin facing up. Bake for 20 minutes, or until the skin blackens and blisters. Put the capsicums in a plastic bag or bowl covered in plastic wrap, allow them to cool and then remove the skin and seeds. Put the flesh of the capsicum into a blender with the balsamic vinegar and 10 basil leaves. Season and blend. Add the strained liquid from the baking tray and the remaining 1 tablespoon of oil to give the capsicums a sauce consistency. Heat the sauce in a large saucepan over a low heat to keep it warm.

Cook the pappardelle in a pot of boiling water until it is *al dente*, then drain the pasta and add it to the sauce. Crumble half the feta through the pasta and toss. Serve garnished with basil leaves and the remaining feta cheese crumbled on top.

vine leaf chicken   serves 4

250 g (9 oz) cherry tomatoes
1 handful mint leaves
1 handful flat-leaf (Italian) parsley
250 g (9 oz/1 cup) firm ricotta cheese
1 egg
4 x 200 g (7 oz) boneless skinless
  chicken breasts
12 whole vine leaves in brine
250 ml (9 fl oz/1 cup) white wine
1 lemon, juiced
2 handfuls mixed baby leaf salad
2 tablespoons extra virgin olive oil

Preheat the oven to 200°C (400°F/ Gas 6). Purée the tomatoes, 8 mint leaves and the parsley in a food processor. Stir through the ricotta cheese with the egg and set aside. Pound the chicken pieces until they are 5 mm (1/4 in) thick. Put each chicken piece onto three overlapping vine leaves and spread the ricotta cheese mixture over the surface of each one. Season with freshly ground black pepper and a little sea salt. Roll up and secure with a toothpick. Arrange the parcels in a baking dish. Pour over the white wine and lemon juice and cover with foil. Bake for 30 minutes. Remove and allow to cool. Unwrap the parcels and lay a vine leaf on a serving plate and top with salad. Slice the chicken and arrange on top of the salad with the remaining mint leaves. Drizzle with the extra virgin olive oil.

tomato and basil soup

3 tablespoons olive oil

2 red onions, thinly sliced

2 garlic cloves, finely chopped

1 kg (2 lb 4 oz) roughly chopped
   ripe tomatoes

1 litre (35 fl oz/4 cups) vegetable
   stock (basics)

15 large basil leaves

1 tablespoon soy sauce

Heat the olive oil, onions and garlic in a large saucepan over medium heat. Sauté until the onion is transparent, then add the tomatoes and cook for 5 minutes. Add the vegetable stock. Bring almost to the boil, then reduce the heat and simmer for 20 minutes. Remove from the heat and allow to cool. Add the basil and soy sauce. Transfer to a blender and blend until smooth. Return the soup to the saucepan, season to taste with sea salt and freshly ground black pepper and heat to serve.

fettuccine with chilli, corn and prawns

serves 4

2 tablespoons olive oil

2 small red chillies, seeded and finely chopped

1 teaspoon smoked paprika

3 spring onions (scallions), thinly sliced

3 corn cobs, kernels removed

3 vine-ripened tomatoes, finely chopped

20 raw medium prawns (shrimp), peeled and deveined with tails intact

400 g (14 oz) fettuccine

2 handfuls baby rocket (arugula) leaves

2 tablespoons extra virgin olive oil

Bring a large pot of salted water to the boil.

Heat the olive oil in a large frying pan over medium heat and add the chillies, paprika and spring onions. Stir-fry for 1 minute, then add the corn and tomatoes. Cook for a couple of minutes, or until the corn is soft and a deep golden colour. Add the prawns and continue to cook for 2–3 minutes, or until the prawns are pink and curled up. Remove from the heat and season to taste with sea salt and freshly ground black pepper.

Add the fettuccine to the boiling water and cook until *al dente*. Drain and return to the hot pot. Pour in the corn and prawn sauce, add the rocket leaves and stir together. Divide among four bowls and drizzle with the extra virgin olive oil.

warm vegetables with white beans

serves 4

125 ml (4 fl oz/$\frac{1}{2}$ cup) olive oil
6 slices pancetta, finely chopped
1 red onion, finely diced
2 garlic cloves, crushed
1 teaspoon finely chopped rosemary
  leaves
2 celery stalks, thinly sliced
1 large eggplant (aubergine), finely
  diced
2 red capsicums (peppers), finely diced
400 g (14 oz) tin chopped tomatoes
1 orange, zest grated, juiced
400 g (14 oz) tin cannellini beans,
  drained and rinsed
2 tablespoons roughly chopped
  flat-leaf (Italian) parsley
2 tablespoons extra virgin olive oil
basil leaves, to serve
crusty bread, to serve

Heat the oil in a large frying pan over medium heat and add the pancetta, onion, garlic and rosemary. Cook until the onion begins to soften and then add the celery, eggplant and capsicums. When the eggplant begins to soften add the chopped tomatoes, orange zest and orange juice. Cover and continue to cook over low heat for 30 minutes. Add the cannellini beans and cook for a further 1–2 minutes, then fold in the parsley and spoon into a serving dish. Drizzle with the extra virgin olive oil. Scatter with basil leaves. Serve with warm crusty bread or as a side dish to roast lamb.

fisherman's soup

serves 4

2 tablespoons olive oil

1 onion, thinly sliced

2 garlic cloves, crushed

pinch saffron threads

1 fennel bulb, finely diced

3 ripe tomatoes, finely chopped

1.5 litres (52 fl oz/6 cups) fish stock
   (basics)

500 g (1 lb 2 oz) ling fillets, cut into
   bite-sized pieces

lemon, to serve

extra virgin olive oil, to serve

crusty bread, to serve

Heat the olive oil in a large saucepan and add the onion, garlic and saffron. Cook over low to medium heat until the onion is soft but not brown. Add the fennel and cook for a couple of minutes before adding the tomatoes. Add the fish stock and simmer for 10 minutes. Add the ling fillet pieces and simmer for a further few minutes, or until the fish is cooked through. Season to taste with sea salt and freshly ground black pepper and serve with some lemon, a drizzle of extra virgin olive oil and warm crusty bread.

risoni with sweet and sour capsicum

1 red onion, thinly sliced
2 red capsicums (peppers), thickly sliced
2 tablespoons balsamic vinegar
2 tablespoons soft brown sugar
250 g (9 oz/1¼ cups) risoni
2 large ripe tomatoes, roughly chopped
10 large basil leaves, roughly torn
150 g (5½ oz) baby rocket (arugula) leaves
4 tablespoons extra virgin olive oil

Preheat the oven to 180°C (350°F/ Gas 4). Put the onion, capsicum, vinegar and sugar in an ovenproof dish and toss the together. Season the vegetables with a little sea salt, cover with foil and bake in the oven for 30 minutes.

Remove the baking dish and allow the vegetables to cool. Cook the risoni in a large pan of rapidly boiling water for 10 minutes, or until *al dente*, then drain it well.

Put the risoni in a large bowl with the capsicum mixture, tomatoes, basil and rocket and toss to combine. Season to taste and drizzle with the extra virgin olive oil.

prawns with fresh tomato sauce

serves 4

2 tablespoons olive oil

5 garlic cloves, thinly sliced

5 spring onions (scallions), peeled and thinly sliced

5 makrut (kaffir lime) leaves

5 vine-ripened tomatoes, finely chopped

20 g (3/4 oz) palm sugar, shaved

4 tablespoons lime juice

1 tablespoon fish sauce

20 large raw prawns (shrimp), peeled and deveined with tails intact

To make the tomato sauce, heat the oil in a saucepan over medium heat and cook the garlic and spring onions until golden brown. Add the makrut leaves and tomatoes and simmer for about 5 minutes, or until the tomatoes are soft. Add the sugar, lime juice and fish sauce and simmer for a further 10 minutes. Remove from the heat.

Heat a non-stick frying pan over high heat and sear the prawns for 2–3 minutes, or until pink on both sides and beginning to curl up. Serve with the tomato sauce.

tomato risotto

1 litre (35 fl oz/4 cups) chicken stock
   (basics)
40 g (1½ oz) butter
1 tablespoon olive oil
1 red onion, diced
225 g (8 oz/1 cup) risotto rice
125 ml (4 fl oz/½ cup) white wine
8 ripe tomatoes, halved, seeds
   removed, cut into bite-sized chunks
100 g (3½ oz/1 cup) grated parmesan
   cheese
olive oil, extra, to drizzle
basil leaves, to serve

Heat the chicken stock in a saucepan. Heat the butter and olive oil in a large heavy-based saucepan over medium heat. Add the onion and sauté until soft and transparent. Add the risotto rice and stir for 1 minute, or until the grains are coated and glossy. Add the white wine, simmer and stir until absorbed. Add 250 ml (9 fl oz/1 cup) of stock and stir until absorbed. Add the tomatoes and 250 ml (9 fl oz/ 1 cup) of stock and stir until the stock is absorbed. Stir in 250 ml (9 fl oz/ 1 cup) of stock. When absorbed, test if the rice is *al dente*. If undercooked, add the remaining stock and simmer until the stock has reduced and the rice is coated in a creamy sauce. Fold the parmesan cheese through, then put into bowls. Serve with a drizzle of olive oil and a sprinkling of basil leaves.

fish, clam and herb soup

serves 4

500 g (1 lb 2 oz) live clams (vongole)
in the shell
4 tablespoons olive oil
2 onions, finely chopped
2 garlic cloves, crushed
1/2 teaspoon thyme
1/2 teaspoon smoked paprika
14 sage leaves, 2 finely chopped
1/2 teaspoon finely chopped rosemary
125 ml (4 fl oz/1/2 cup) white wine
4 large ripe tomatoes, finely diced
2 large potatoes, finely diced
2 tablespoons tomato paste
(concentrated purée)
500 g (1 lb 2 oz) white fish fillets, cut
into bite-sized pieces
3 tablespoons finely chopped flat-leaf
(Italian) parsley

Soak the clams in water for about 10 minutes, discarding any that don't close when tapped.

Heat half the oil in a saucepan over medium heat. Add the onions, garlic, thyme, paprika, chopped sage and rosemary. Cook until the onions are transparent then add the wine and clams. Cover and cook for 1 minute. When the clams have opened, remove and set aside. Add the tomatoes, potatoes, paste and 750 ml (26 fl oz/3 cups) of water. Simmer for 10 minutes, then add the fish and cook for another 5 minutes.

Meanwhile, fry the whole sage leaves in the remaining oil until crispy. Add the parsley and clams to the soup then garnish with the crispy sage leaves.

steak with onion salsa serves 4

2 large red onions, thickly sliced
2 ripe tomatoes
2 handfuls flat-leaf (Italian) parsley
10 oregano leaves
1 tablespoon balsamic vinegar
3 tablespoons extra virgin olive oil
4 x 180 g (6 oz) fillet steaks

Preheat a barbecue hotplate or chargrill pan to high heat. To make the onion salsa, grill (broil) the onion until it is quite blackened on both sides. Remove and put on a chopping board. Put the tomatoes on the barbecue. Roughly chop the cooked onion. Transfer the onion to a bowl. Once the tomatoes begin to blacken, turn over and cook for a further minute. Put them in the bowl with the onions and roughly chop with a sharp knife or a pair of kitchen scissors. Add the parsley, oregano, vinegar and extra virgin olive oil. Season with sea salt and freshly ground black pepper to taste and toss the salsa ingredients together.

Meanwhile, put the steaks on the barbecue and sear for 2–3 minutes. Turn over and cook for a further minute. Remove from the barbecue and set aside to rest. Serve with the onion salsa.

tuna with tomato and olives

serves 4

20 cherry tomatoes, quartered
20 basil leaves
32 small black olives
2 tablespoons balsamic vinegar
4 tablespoons extra virgin olive oil
2 teaspoons olive oil
4 x 200 g (7 oz) tuna steaks
green leaf salad, to serve

Put the tomatoes, basil leaves, black olives, balsamic vinegar and extra virgin olive oil into a bowl and mix.

Heat the olive oil in a frying pan over high heat. Add the tuna steaks and sear them on one side for 1 minute. Turn the tuna steaks over, reduce the heat to medium and cook them for a further 3–4 minutes.

Put the tuna onto warmed plates and top with the tomatoes and olives. Serve with a green leaf salad.

chilli mussels

2 kg (4 lb 8 oz) black mussels
3 tablespoons olive oil
1 teaspoon red chilli flakes
3 garlic cloves, finely chopped
15 saffron threads
1 kg (2 lb 4 oz) tinned peeled tomatoes
60 g (2¼ oz/¼ cup) tomato paste
  (concentrated purée)
185 ml (6 fl oz/¾ cup) white wine
80 g (2¾ oz) roughly chopped flat-leaf
  (Italian) parsley
crusty bread, to serve

Clean the mussels under cold running water, scrubbing them to remove any barnacles or bits of hairy 'beard'. Discard any that are open and that do not close when you tap them.

Heat the olive oil in a large saucepan over medium heat and sauté the chilli, garlic and saffron for 1 minute. Add the tomatoes, breaking them up as you stir. Mix in the tomato paste and cook for 10 minutes. Bring to the boil and add the mussels. Cover and cook for 3 minutes, or until they have all opened, discarding any that haven't. Reduce the heat to a simmer and remove the mussels to four warmed bowls. Add the white wine to the pan and cook for another 2 minutes before ladling the hot broth over the mussels. Garnish with the parsley and serve with warm crusty bread.

lamb cutlets with mint salsa

serves 4

1 Lebanese (short) cucumber,
  finely diced
2 tablespoons finely diced red onion
2 tablespoons balsamic vinegar
1 tablespoon extra virgin olive oil
3 handfuls mint
1 tablespoon caster (superfine) sugar
1 tablespoon oil
12 small lamb cutlets
roast sweet potato (basics)

To make the salsa, put the cucumber, red onion, vinegar and olive oil in a small bowl and toss them together. Finely chop the mint leaves, sprinkling them with sugar halfway through chopping. Add the mint and sugar to the bowl and stir them into the salsa.

Heat the oil in a frying pan and sear the lamb cutlets on one side until golden brown. Turn over and cook the other side for another 2–4 minutes, depending on how thick the cutlets are. Remove the pan from the heat, season the cutlets and allow to rest.

Divide among four plates and add some salsa to each cutlet. Serve with roast sweet potato.

seared tuna with red capsicums and anchovies

serves 4

2 tablespoons vegetable oil
2 red capsicums (peppers)
4 anchovies, roughly chopped
1 handful flat-leaf (Italian) parsley
12 basil leaves
4 tablespoons extra virgin olive oil
4 x 150 g (51/2 oz) tuna steaks
2 handfuls baby English spinach leaves
1 tablespoon balsamic vinegar

Heat half the vegetable oil in a frying pan over high heat. Add the capsicums and sear, turning occasionally, until they are blistered on all sides. Transfer to a bowl and cover with plastic wrap. When the capsicums are cool, remove the seeds, stalk and any skin that rubs off easily, making sure you catch the liquid in the bowl.

Slice the capsicums into thin strips and put into another bowl. Strain the liquid from the original bowl over them. Add the anchovies, parsley, basil and extra virgin olive oil. Season with freshly ground black pepper. Heat the remaining vegetable oil in the frying pan over a high heat. Add the tuna steaks and sear on one side for 1 minute. Turn the tuna over, reduce the heat to medium and cook for a further 3–4 minutes. Divide the spinach among four plates, top with tuna and spoon over the capsicum salad. Drizzle with a little balsamic vinegar and serve.

mussels with rouille serves 4

2 kg (4 lb 8 oz) mussels
2 tablespoons olive oil
1 onion, finely chopped
2 garlic cloves, crushed
3 large ripe tomatoes, diced
1 bay leaf
1 fennel bulb, thinly sliced
1 pinch saffron threads
1 teaspoon sea salt
250 ml (9 fl oz/1 cup) white wine
15 g (1/2 oz) flat-leaf (Italian) parsley
rouille (basics)
crusty white bread, to serve

Clean the mussels under cold running water, scrubbing them to remove any barnacles or bits of hairy 'beard'. Discard any that are open and that do not close when you tap them.

Put the oil, onion and garlic into a saucepan and cook them over low heat until the onion is transparent. Add the tomatoes, bay leaf, fennel and saffron, season with the sea salt and simmer for 10 minutes. Pour in the white wine, bring the sauce to the boil and add the mussels. Cover with the lid and cook for a few minutes, shaking the pan once or twice. Check that all the mussels have opened. Discard any that remain closed.

Divide the mussels among four bowls, sprinkle with the parsley and serve with the rouille and crusty white bread.

lamb shanks with parsnip, lemon and herbs
serves 4

4 red onions, quartered
6 garlic cloves, thinly sliced
4 sprigs thyme
4 lamb shanks (about 1.2 kg/2 lb 12 oz)
1 large parsnip, peeled
8 sage leaves
250 ml (9 fl oz/1 cup) veal stock
  (basics)

gremolata
1 tablespoon small capers, rinsed
  and drained
1 garlic clove, crushed
1 lemon, zested
3 handfuls flat-leaf (Italian) parsley
  leaves

Preheat the oven to 200°C (400°F/ Gas 6). Make a bed of the red onions, garlic and thyme in a deep casserole dish. Put the shanks on top, then arrange the parsnip and sage leaves over them and season well. Pour over the veal stock and cover with a lid or foil. Bake for 1 hour, then uncover and bake for a further 30 minutes, or until the meat is pulling away from the bones.

To make the gremolata, put the capers, garlic, lemon zest and parsley leaves on a chopping board and chop them together finely with a sharp knife. Serve sprinkled over the lamb shanks.

roasted tuna with fennel and tomato

serves 4

4 ripe tomatoes
2 garlic cloves, thinly sliced
14–16 sprigs thyme
75 g (2¹/₂ oz/¹/₂ cup) small black olives
1 x 500 g (1 lb 2 oz) tuna fillet
2 tablespoons freshly ground black pepper
125 ml (4 fl oz/¹/₂ cup) olive oil
15 basil leaves, roughly torn
1 fennel bulb, sliced paper thin
2 tablespoons extra virgin olive oil

Preheat the oven to 200°C (400°F/ Gas 6). Bring a saucepan of salted water to the boil. Make a small X-shaped incision at the base of each tomato and put in the boiling water for 1 minute. Remove with a slotted spoon and put in a bowl to cool.

Lay the garlic and thyme over the base of a deep roasting tin. Scatter with the olives. Roll the tuna fillet in the ground black pepper. Place over the thyme. Drizzle with the olive oil. Season with sea salt. Seal the roasting tin with foil. Bake for 25 minutes.

Peel the tomatoes. Put in a bowl. Using a sharp knife, chop while still in the bowl into bite-sized pieces. Season with sea salt. Add the basil leaves. Toss. Remove the tuna from the oven. Remove the olives from the roasting tin and add to the tomato mixture along with 1 or 2 tablespoons of the cooking liquid. On a plate, layer the fennel with the tomato. Top with several thin slices of tuna. Drizzle with extra virgin olive oil. Garnish with thyme from the baking tray.

roast beef

2 kg (4 lb 8 oz) rib joint of beef
olive oil
1 teaspoon sea salt
1 teaspoon freshly ground black pepper

Preheat the oven to 220°C (425°F/ Gas 7). Stand the beef in a roasting tin and allow to come to room temperature. Rub the beef all over with olive oil and season the sea salt and freshly ground black pepper. Roast for 20 minutes, then reduce the heat to 180°C (350°F/Gas 4) and roast for a further 1 hour. Transfer the beef to a warm platter, cover with aluminium foil and rest it for 15 minutes before carving. Serve with roasted vegetables, mustard and horseradish and Yorkshire puddings.

swordfish with prosciutto

serves 4

8 kalamata olives, pitted
60 g (2 1/4 oz) butter, softened
2 tablespoons light olive oil
4 slices prosciutto
400 g (14 oz) kipfler (fingerling) or salad
    potatoes, thinly sliced
6 spring onions (scallions), trimmed
    and sliced on the diagonal
375 ml (13 fl oz/1 1/2 cups) white wine
4 x 200 g (7 oz) swordfish steaks
green salad or steamed green beans,
    to serve

Finely chop the olives and stir into the butter. Heat the oil in a large frying pan over medium heat, add the prosciutto and fry until crisp. Once the prosciutto is cooked, move it to the side of the pan and put in the potatoes and spring onions. When the potatoes begin to soften, add the white wine and the swordfish steaks, arranging the swordfish on top of the potatoes and putting a piece of cooked prosciutto on top of each steak. Cover the pan and simmer for 12 minutes.

Check that the fish is cooked through and then serve the swordfish and potatoes on warmed serving plates. Divide the olive butter among the steaks and spoon the wine sauce over the top. Serve with a green salad or steamed green beans.

lamb cutlets with couscous salad

60 g (2¹/₄ oz/¹/₃ cup) couscous
5 g (¹/₈ oz) butter
2 teaspoons ground cumin
3 ripe roma (plum) tomatoes, diced
1 Lebanese (short) cucumber, diced
¹/₂ red onion, finely diced
1 handful flat-leaf (Italian) parsley,
   roughly chopped
1 tablespoon balsamic vinegar
3 tablespoons extra virgin olive oil
12 lamb cutlets

Put the couscous in a bowl and add the butter, cumin and 125 ml (4 fl oz/ ¹/₂ cup) of boiling water. Cover and allow to soak for 2–3 minutes.

Meanwhile, combine the tomatoes, cucumber, onion, parsley, vinegar and olive oil in a large bowl. Season with sea salt and freshly ground black pepper and stir until all the ingredients are coated in the dressing. Fluff the couscous with a fork, then toss it through the salad.

Barbecue or grill (broil) the cutlets for 2–3 minutes on each side. Remove from the heat, season with sea salt and rest for 1 minute. Spoon the salad onto four plates and top with the cutlets.

chilli tomato blue-eye cod

serves 4

4 tablespoons olive oil

4 green chillies, seeded and finely
  chopped

1 teaspoon paprika

1 tablespoon finely grated fresh ginger

1 red onion, thinly sliced

1 tablespoon soft brown sugar

250 g (9 oz) cherry tomatoes

4 x 200 g (7 oz) blue-eye cod fillets

10 sprigs thyme

40 g (1½ oz) butter

1 handful coriander (cilantro) leaves

steamed green beans, to serve

Heat the olive oil in a deep heavy-based frying pan over medium heat and add the green chillies, paprika, ginger and red onion. Cook for 5 minutes, then add the brown sugar, 200 ml (7 fl oz) of water and the cherry tomatoes. Continue to cook for a further 5 minutes and then add the fish fillets and cover with the thyme sprigs. Simmer for 5 minutes, or until the fish is cooked through. Remove the fish fillets and place on four warmed serving plates. Add the butter to the sauce and stir until it has melted into the tomatoes. Spoon the tomato sauce over the fish and garnish with coriander. Serve with steamed green beans.

sausage and white bean stew

serves 4

2 x 400 g (14 oz) tins cannellini beans, drained and rinsed
5 ripe roma (plum) tomatoes, chopped
400 g (14 oz) tin chopped tomatoes
2 leeks, roughly chopped
8 garlic cloves, peeled
1 tablespoon thyme leaves
250 ml (9 fl oz/1 cup) white wine
350 g (12 oz) good-quality spicy thick sausages
1 large handful roughly chopped parsley
crusty bread, to serve

Preheat the oven to 180°C (350°F/ Gas 4). Put the beans, all the tomatoes, the leeks, garlic, thyme and white wine into a casserole or ovenproof dish.

Prick the skins of the sausages with a fork and then sear them in a frying pan over high heat until they are browned on all sides. Cut the sausages into bite-size pieces and put them into the casserole dish. Lightly stir together, then cover the dish with a lid or foil and put in the oven for 1 hour.

Sprinkle with the parsley before serving with warm crusty bread.

ocean trout in tomato and orange marinade

4 x 150 g (5¹/2 oz) skinless ocean trout
   fillets, boned
2 tablespoons olive oil
1 handful flat-leaf (Italian) parsley
1 lemon, zested, juiced
1 orange, zested, juiced
500 g (1 lb 2 oz) vine-ripened
   tomatoes, finely diced
15 g (¹/2 oz/¹/4 cup) finely chopped
   spring onions (scallions)
1 tablespoon small salted capers,
   rinsed and drained
spinach leaves, to serve

Slice the trout into 4 cm (1¹/2 in) wide slices. Heat half the oil in a large, heavy-based frying pan over medium heat and sear the trout for 1 minute on all sides. Put on a serving dish and season with sea salt and freshly ground black pepper.

Scatter the parsley over the fish. Add the citrus juice and zest, tomatoes, spring onions and capers to the pan and cook for 1 minute. Pour over the fish and drizzle with the remaining olive oil. Allow to sit for 1 hour.

Serve the trout fillets on a salad of spinach leaves with a spoonful of the marinade.

lamb shanks with white beans

serves 4

125 g (4$\frac{1}{2}$ oz/1 cup) plain (all-purpose) flour
4 lamb shanks (about 1.2 kg/2 lb 12 oz)
160 ml (5$\frac{1}{4}$ fl oz) olive oil
1 large red onion, thinly sliced
2 garlic cloves, crushed
1 teaspoon rosemary
1 celery stalk, diced
2 carrots, thinly sliced into rounds
200 g (7 oz/1 cup) dried haricot beans, soaked overnight
500 ml (17 fl oz/2 cups) veal stock (basics)
125 ml (4 fl oz/$\frac{1}{2}$ cup) dry Marsala
horseradish gremolata (basics)

Preheat the oven to 200°C (400°F/ Gas 6). Put the flour in a plastic bag, add the shanks and toss until well coated.

Heat half the olive oil in a casserole dish. Add the shanks and turn until they are browned on all sides. Remove from the heat and set aside.

Heat the remaining oil in a frying pan over medium heat. Add the onion, garlic and rosemary and cook until the onion is soft and lightly golden. Spoon the onion, celery, carrots and soaked beans over the lamb shanks, then add the stock and Marsala. Cover and bake in the oven for 2 hours, moving the shanks around in the liquid halfway through. Remove from the oven. Serve with a sprinkle of the horseradish gremolata.

swordfish with a pine nut sauce

1 slice white bread, crusts removed
60 g (2¼ oz/heaped ⅓ cup) pine nuts
½ garlic clove
2 tablespoons lemon juice
1 tablespoon olive oil
4 x 175 g (6 oz) swordfish steaks
salad of tomatoes, red onion and basil

Soak the bread in cold water and then squeeze it dry. Put the pine nuts, bread, garlic and lemon juice in a food processor. Process to a smooth paste. Add 60 ml (2 fl oz/¼ cup) of water to thin it to a pourable consistency.

Heat the olive oil in a large frying pan over high heat. Sear the swordfish steaks on one side for 2 minutes, or until golden brown and then turn them over and reduce the heat. Cook the other side for a further 2–3 minutes, or until the steaks are cooked through — they should feel firm when pressed.

Spoon the sauce over the fish and serve with a salad of tomatoes, red onion and basil.

roast chicken

1.8 kg (4 lb) chicken
1 handful lemon thyme
1 lemon, halved
1 white onion, cut into quarters
1 tablespoon chilled butter
2 lemons, extra

Preheat the oven to 200°C (400°F/ Gas 6). Rinse the chicken under cold running water and pat dry with paper towels. Scatter most of the lemon thyme over the base of a roasting tin. Generously rub the chicken skin with salt and put the chicken on top of the herbs, breast-side up.

Put the onion and lemon inside the chicken cavity along with a few sprigs of lemon thyme. Place your finger under the skin that covers the breast and slightly pull it away from the flesh. Put the butter under the skin. Repeat on the other side.

Bake for 1 hour 15 minutes, or until it is cooked through. To test if the chicken is cooked, pull a leg away from the body — the juices that run out should be clear and not pink. When the chicken is cooked, squeeze 2 lemons over it and bake for a further 5 minutes. Remove from the oven and allow the chicken to rest for 10 minutes before carving. Arrange the chicken pieces on a serving platter and pour some of the lemony pan juices over them.

seaside risoni

210 g (7¹/2 oz/1 cup) risoni
40 g (1¹/2 oz) butter
12 saffron threads
2 garlic cloves, crushed
400 g (14 oz) tin chopped tomatoes
500 ml (17 fl oz/2 cups) white wine
12 large raw prawns (shrimp), peeled
  and deveined with tails intact
16 black mussels, cleaned
2 tablespoons finely chopped
  preserved lemon
1 handful flat-leaf (Italian) parsley
  leaves

Bring a large pot of salted water to the boil. Cook the risoni until it is *al dente,* then drain and set aside.

In a deep, wide frying pan or wok, heat the butter, saffron and garlic until the butter begins to bubble. Add the tomatoes and white wine and simmer for 2 minutes. Add the risoni, prawns and mussels to the tomato mixture and cover the pan with a lid. Simmer until the mussels have opened, discarding any that don't. Remove from the heat and divide the mixture between four warm pasta bowls. Garnish with preserved lemon and parsley leaves.

sage and parmesan veal chops

serves 4

4 sage leaves
80 g (2³/₄ oz/1 cup) fresh breadcrumbs
35 g (1¹/₄ oz/¹/₃ cup) grated parmesan
cheese
2 tablespoons roughly chopped
flat-leaf (Italian) parsley
¹/₄ teaspoon salt
2 eggs
4 x 200 g (7 oz) veal chops
40 g (1¹/₂ oz) butter
2 tablespoons olive oil
lemon wedges, to serve
green salad, to serve

Preheat the oven to 200°C (400°F/ Gas 6). Put the sage, breadcrumbs, parmesan and parsley into a food processor. Season with the sea salt and some freshly ground black pepper. Process until fine breadcrumbs form. Beat the eggs in a bowl and set aside. Dip each cutlet into the egg mixture, then press firmly into the breadcrumbs. Heat the butter and olive oil in an ovenproof frying pan over medium to high heat. Cook the cutlets for 2 minutes on each side, then bake for 12 minutes. Serve with lemon wedges and a green salad.

salsa snapper

2 ripe tomatoes, finely chopped
1 Lebanese (short) cucumber,
   finely chopped
1/2 red onion, finely diced
2 large red chillies, seeded and
   thinly sliced
1 handful coriander (cilantro) leaves
2 teaspoons ground cumin
2 teaspoons fish sauce
2 tablespoons lemon juice
4 tablespoons olive oil
4 x 200 g (7 oz) snapper fillets, skin on
2 tablespoons vegetable oil

Preheat the oven to 180°C (350°F/ Gas 4). Lightly stir the tomatoes, cucumber, onion, chillies, coriander leaves, cumin, fish sauce, lemon juice and olive oil together in a small bowl. Season to taste with sea salt and freshly ground black pepper.

Rinse the fish fillets and pat dry with paper towels. Heat the vegetable oil in a large ovenproof frying pan over a high heat. Season the fillets liberally with sea salt and put them, skin side down, in the hot pan. Sear the fillets for 1–2 minutes, or until the skin is crisply golden and then turn them over.

Put the fillets in the frying pan in the oven and bake for 8 minutes, then transfer the fillets to a serving dish. Cover with a spoonful of the salsa and serve immediately.

osso bucco

serves 4

4 x 4 cm (1½ in) thick slices of veal
   hind shank
40 g (1½ oz/⅓ cup) plain (all-purpose)
   flour
1 teaspoon sea salt
4 tablespoons olive oil
1 leek, washed and thinly sliced
1 celery stalk, finely chopped
400 g (14 oz) tin chopped tomatoes
250 ml (9 fl oz/1 cup) red wine
1 orange, zested and juiced
rocket (arugula), to serve
polenta (basics), to serve

Put the veal shanks, flour and sea salt into a clean plastic bag and toss until each shank is lightly coated in the flour. Heat the olive oil in a large stoveproof casserole dish over medium heat and brown the shanks, two at a time, on all sides. Remove and set aside. Add the leek and celery and cook until the leek is soft. Add the tomatoes and cook over high heat for 5 minutes. Add the wine, orange zest and juice. Stir to combine, then add the shanks. Cover the casserole dish and reduce to a simmer. Cook for 1½ hours. Serve with a rocket and warm polenta.

blue-eye cod with saffron and capers

4 roma (plum) tomatoes, thickly diced
1 leek, washed and thinly sliced
10 saffron threads
1 tablespoon salted capers, rinsed
   and drained
250 ml (9 fl oz/1 cup) white wine
4 x 200 g (7 oz) blue-eye cod fillets
20 g (3/4 oz) butter
2 tablespoons small black olives
1 handful flat-leaf (Italian) parsley leaves
boiled potatoes, to serve

Preheat the oven to 180°C (350°F/ Gas 4). Put the tomatoes in the bottom of a stoveproof casserole or roasting tin over medium heat. Top with the leek, then sprinkle the saffron and capers over. Add the wine and bring to the boil. Reduce the heat to a simmer and cook for a further 10 minutes. Add the fish, then season lightly with sea salt and freshly ground black pepper and dot with the butter. Cover and bake for 15 minutes.

Remove and place the fish on serving plates. Spoon over the sauce, then garnish with the olives and parsley. Serve with boiled potatoes.

fillet steak with an onion and mushroom sauce serves 4

10 g (1/4 oz) dried porcini mushrooms
2 red onions, cut into eighths
   lengthways
250 ml (9 fl oz/1 cup) red wine
1 garlic clove, crushed
1 tablespoon olive oil
4 x 175 g (6 oz) fillet steaks
100 g (3 1/2 oz) oyster mushrooms
40 g (1 1/2 oz) butter
borlotti bean and chopped basil salad,
   to serve

Soak the dried mushrooms in 250 ml (9 fl oz/1 cup) of boiling water, then drain, reserving the liquid.

Put the onions in a large saucepan and add the wine, garlic and the mushroom soaking liquid. Slice the soaked mushrooms thinly and add them to the saucepan. Bring everything to the boil, then reduce the heat to a low simmer. Cook for 30 minutes, or until the liquid has almost evaporated.

Heat a heavy-based frying pan over high heat and add the oil. As it begins to smoke, add the steaks and sear them until the uncooked surface looks slightly bloody. Turn each steak over and cook for a further minute before taking the pan off the heat. Season the steaks and let them sit for a few minutes in the pan.

Add the oyster mushrooms and butter to the onion mix. Cook for a further 1 minute. Serve the steaks on warmed plates with a salad of borlotti beans and chopped basil, and spoon the onion sauce over the steaks.

capsicum and potato stew
with saffron
serves 4

40 g (1½ oz) butter
2 red onions, diced
2 garlic cloves, crushed
1 large pinch saffron threads
400 g (14 oz) tin chopped tomatoes
1 teaspoon sugar
700 g (1 lb 9 oz) waxy potatoes, cut
  into bite-sized pieces
1 red capsicum (pepper), cut into
  thick strips
1 teaspoon thyme leaves
1 large handful coriander (cilantro)
  leaves
30 g (1 oz) chives, finely chopped

Heat the butter, onions, garlic and saffron together in a large saucepan over medium heat. When the onions are soft and transparent, add the tomatoes, sugar and 500 ml (17 fl oz/ 2 cups) of water. Cover with a lid and simmer for 10 minutes. Add the potatoes, capsicum and thyme, then cover and simmer for a further 35 minutes. Season with sea salt and freshly ground black pepper and serve sprinkled with the coriander and chives.

red mullet with tomato and fennel sauce

serves 4

2 teaspoons sea salt
2 teaspoons fennel seeds
20 mint leaves
1 tablespoon olive oil
4 ripe tomatoes, finely chopped
125 ml (4 fl oz/1/2 cup) white wine
2 small fennel bulbs, thinly sliced
4 x 175 g (6 oz) red mullet, gutted
  and scaled
2 tablespoons extra virgin olive oil

Preheat the oven to 180°C (350°F/ Gas 4). Put the sea salt, fennel seeds and mint leaves in a mortar and pestle or small blender and grind them together. When the leaves and seeds have begun to break down, add the oil to make a thin paste.

Put half of the tomatoes, the wine and half the fennel into a casserole dish. Rinse the mullet in cold water and dry with paper towels. Rub with the fennel paste, then put the fish on top of the tomatoes. Stuff some of the remaining fennel into the fish cavities and scatter the rest over the fish, along with the remaining tomatoes. Cover with a lid and bake for 25 minutes.

To serve, carefully remove the whole fish and put them on warmed serving plates. Spoon the sauce over the fish, season with freshly ground black pepper and drizzle with extra virgin olive oil.

linguine with prawns and fresh herbs

serves 4

400 g (14 oz) linguine
100 ml (3¹/₃ fl oz) light olive oil
3 garlic cloves, crushed and finely
  chopped
16 raw king prawns (shrimp), peeled
  and deveined, with tails intact
250 g (9 oz) cherry tomatoes, halved
1 handful flat-leaf (Italian) parsley,
  roughly chopped
12 basil leaves, torn
30 g (1 oz) chives
juice of 1 lemon

Bring a large pot of salted water to the boil. Add the linguine and cook in rapidly boiling water until *al dente*. Meanwhile, put the olive oil in a frying pan and heat over medium heat. Add the garlic, stir briefly, then add the prawns. Fry the prawns until they are pink on both sides and have begun to curl up. Add the cherry tomatoes and cook for a further 1 minute. Remove from the heat.

Strain the cooked linguine and return it to the pot. Add the prawn and tomato mixture, herbs and lemon juice. Toss together. Season with sea salt and freshly ground black pepper.

pastry twists panettone fingers with rhubarb spiced biscotti with marsala mascarpone chocolate pots with chocolate wafers ice cream shots with sweet liquers fresh fig tarts chocolate truffles florentines tiny tiramisu chocolate creams fig surprise chocolate samosas chocolate caramel 'brûlées' strawberries with nutty filo chocolate brownies figs in sauterne with crème fraîche parfait chocolate pudding

04 sweets

chocolate nut meringues with cream and berries rich chocolate cake chocolate marquise strawberry rice pudding mini chocolate cakes chocolate slice crème anglaise butterfly cakes hazelnut meringue with berries mini danish coconut and white chocolate

pastry twists

2 teaspoons ground cinnamon
55 g (2 oz/1/4 cup) caster (superfine) sugar
1/2 sheet ready-prepared puff pastry
15 g (1/2 oz) unsalted butter, melted

Place the cinnamon and sugar in a small bowl and stir to combine. Cut the pastry into 12 x 5 mm (1/4 in) strips, then cut the lengths in half again. Place each of the strips onto a baking tray lined with baking paper, brush with melted butter and sprinkle with some of the cinnamon sugar. Preheat the oven to 160°C (315°F/ Gas 2–3).

Gently twist each strip of pastry to form loose spirals, and sprinkle any remaining sugar over the top. Refrigerate the pastry twists for 10 minutes. Bake for 10–12 minutes, or until lightly golden. Cool on a wire rack. Serve with hot chocolate.

panettone fingers with rhubarb

6 stems rhubarb, trimmed
1/2 teaspoon grated fresh ginger
1 teaspoon finely chopped orange zest
4 tablespoons orange juice
1/2 vanilla bean, split and scraped
55 g (2 oz/1/4 cup) soft brown sugar
15 g (1/2 oz) unsalted butter
12 fingers panettone, cut into 12 x
    2 cm (5 x 3/4 in) lengths
icing (confectioners') sugar, for dusting

Preheat the oven to 180°C (350°F/ Gas 4). Cut each rhubarb stem into two 12 cm (5 in) lengths. Place the ginger, orange zest, orange juice, vanilla bean, brown sugar and butter in a roasting tin and place in the oven for 1–2 minutes, or until the butter has melted. Remove from the oven and stir to combine. Add the rhubarb and toss together so that the rhubarb is well coated in the sugary mix. Return to the oven for 10 minutes. Turn the rhubarb over and cook for a further 10 minutes. Allow to cool.

Toast each of the panettone fingers under a grill (broiler) until golden and place a strip of rhubarb along each of them. Drizzle with a little of the syrup, sprinkle with icing sugar and serve.

spiced biscotti with marsala mascarpone

makes approximately 120 biscuits

250 g (9 oz/2 cups) plain (all-purpose) flour

230 g (8¹/2 oz/1 cup) caster (superfine) sugar

2 teaspoons baking powder

100 g (3¹/2 oz/heaped ¹/2 cup) sliced dried figs

50 g (1³/4 oz/heaped ¹/4 cup) dried apricots, sliced

150 g (5¹/2 oz/heaped 1²/3 cup) slivered almonds

2 teaspoons chopped lemon zest

¹/4 teaspoon ground cardamom

1 teaspoon ground cinnamon

3 eggs, beaten

marsala mascarpone

200 g (7 oz) mascarpone

2 tablespoons sweet Marsala

1 tablespoon caster (superfine) sugar

Preheat the oven to 180°C (350°F/ Gas 4). Mix the flour, sugar, baking powder, dried fruit, almonds, lemon zest, cardamom and cinnamon in a bowl. Make a well in the centre. Fold in the eggs to make a sticky dough. Divide into four pieces. Roll out each portion of dough to form logs 4 cm (1¹/2 in) in diameter. Place the logs on a baking tray lined with baking paper, leaving space between each log to spread. Bake for 30 minutes. Remove and allow to cool. Reduce the oven temperature to 140°C (275°F/Gas 1).

With a bread knife, cut each of the loaves into thin slices 5 mm (¹/4 in) wide. Lay the biscuits on a baking tray and return to the oven. Bake for 20 minutes, turning the biscuits once. Remove from the oven. Cool on wire racks.

Put the mascarpone, Marsala and caster sugar in a bowl and mix until smooth. Serve the biscotti with the mascarpone mixture.

chocolate pots with chocolate wafers

chocolate pots

300 ml (10¹/2 fl oz) whipping cream
200 g (7 oz) dark chocolate, roughly chopped
1/2 teaspoon natural vanilla extract
1/2 teaspoon ground cardamom
1 egg

chocolate wafers

50 g (1³/4 oz) caster (superfine) sugar
50 g (1³/4 oz) unsalted butter, softened
2 egg whites
40 g (1¹/2 oz) plain (all-purpose) flour
10 g (1/4 oz) dark unsweetened cocoa powder
unsweetened cocoa powder, extra, for dusting

To make the chocolate pots, heat the cream and chocolate in a double boiler over low heat. Allow the chocolate to melt, stirring occasionally. Add a pinch of salt with the vanilla and cardamom. Whisk in the egg. Continue to whisk over low heat until smooth. Pour the mixture into six 125 ml (4 fl oz/1/2 cup) pots and chill for 3 hours.

To make the wafers, whisk the sugar and butter until it is light and creamy. Slowly add the egg whites, then the flour and cocoa. Chill for 1 hour. preheat the oven to 180°C (350°F/Gas 4)

Line a baking sheet with baking paper and, using the back of a spoon, spread 1 tablespoon of the mixture into a thin 10 cm (4 in) circle. Repeat, leaving a little space between wafers. Bake for 15 minutes. Remove from the oven and carefully lift the wafers from the tray with a spatula. Allow to cool on a wire rack. Dust with cocoa powder. Serve with the chocolate pots.

ice cream shots with sweet liqueurs

12 small scoops hazelnut ice cream
60 g (2¹/₄ oz) dark chocolate, grated
100 ml (3¹/₂ fl oz) Frangelico

Divide the ice cream and chocolate among six small glasses and top with the liqueur.

Note – You can use any number of ice cream and liqueur combinations: for example, chocolate ice cream with Tia Maria, coffee ice cream with crème de cacao, or vanilla ice cream with Grand Marnier.

fresh fig tarts

90 g (3^1/$_4$ oz/^{1}/$_4$ cup) honey
120 g (4^1/$_4$ oz) mascarpone
12 pre-baked shortcrust tart cases
   (basics)
3 fresh figs, thinly sliced
40 g (1^1/$_2$ oz/^{1}/$_3$ cup) roughly chopped
   toasted hazelnuts
icing (confectioners') sugar, for dusting

Place the honey and mascarpone in a bowl and blend with a spoon until the mixture is smooth. Spoon into the tart shells. Top with the thinly sliced fresh fig and a scattering of hazelnuts. Sprinkle with icing sugar and serve.

roast lamb

1.5 kg (3 lb 5 oz) leg of lamb
olive oil
5 garlic cloves, halved
35 g (1 oz) rosemary

Preheat the oven to 200°C (400°F/ Gas 6). With the point of a small sharp knife, make several incisions into the skin of a leg of lamb weighing about 1.5 kg (3 lb 5 oz). Rub the surface of the lamb with a little olive oil and then rub salt and pepper into the skin. Press the garlic into the incisions. Scatter the rosemary over the base of a roasting tin and put the lamb on top of it. Bake for 30 minutes, then spoon some of the juices from the tin over the lamb. Bake for a further 40 minutes. Transfer the lamb to a warm platter, cover with aluminium foil and rest it for 15 minutes before carving. Serve with roasted vegetables and fresh mint sauce.

chocolate truffles   makes 25

125 g (4¹/₂ oz) dark chocolate
50 g (1³/₄ oz) sour cream
2 teaspoons finely grated orange zest
¹/₈ teaspoon ground cardamom
30 g (1 oz/¹/₄ cup) unsweetened cocoa
    powder

Place the chocolate in a bowl over a saucepan of simmering water. When the chocolate has melted, fold in the sour cream, orange zest and cardamom. Stir well, then place in the refrigerator for 30 minutes, or until set. Place the cocoa powder in a shallow bowl. Drop a teaspoon at a time of the chocolate mixture into the cocoa. Toss to cover the chocolate with the cocoa, then roll the chocolate into a ball in the palm of your hand, covering the outside with more cocoa. When all the truffles have been rolled, place in an airtight container in the refrigerator until ready to serve.

florentines

2 tablespoons raisins, finely chopped
2 tablespoons finely chopped
  preserved ginger
100 g (3 1/2 oz/1 cup) flaked almonds
100 g (3 1/2 oz) unsalted butter
100 g (3 1/2 oz/1/2 cup) caster (superfine)
  sugar
100 g (3 1/2 oz) dark chocolate

Preheat the oven to 180°C (350°F/ Gas 4). Line two baking trays with baking paper. Add the raisins to a bowl with the ginger and almonds. Melt the butter and sugar in a saucepan over low heat. When the sugar has dissolved, turn up the heat and allow the mixture to bubble for 1 minute. Pour the hot mixture into the bowl and quickly stir to combine all the ingredients. Drop teaspoons of the mixture onto the baking trays, allowing room for the biscuits to spread considerably. Bake for 10 minutes. Allow the biscuits to cool on the trays for 5 minutes before carefully lifting them onto a wire rack to cool completely.

Melt the chocolate and use a pastry brush to paint the chocolate onto the underside of the biscuits.

tiny tiramisu

coffee syrup

2 tablespoons sugar
125 ml (4 fl oz/^{1}/$_2$ cup) strong
  black coffee
125 ml (4 fl oz/^{1}/$_2$ cup) Tia Maria

coffee cupcakes

60 ml (2 fl oz/^{1}/$_4$ cup) strong
  black coffee
2 eggs
100 g (3^1/$_2$ oz) unsalted butter, softened
165 g (5^3/$_4$ oz/^{3}/$_4$ cup) sugar
185 g (6^1/$_2$ oz/1^1/$_2$ cups) plain
  (all-purpose) flour
2 teaspoons baking powder
25 g (1 oz/^{1}/$_4$ cup) ground almonds
30 g (1 oz/^{1}/$_4$ cup) unsweetened
  cocoa powder, for dusting

mascarpone filling

1 tablespoon sugar
2 egg yolks
125 ml (4 fl oz/^{1}/$_2$ cup) Marsala
250 g (9 oz) mascarpone

Make a coffee syrup by bringing the sugar and coffee to the boil in a small saucepan. Simmer for 5 minutes. Remove, allow to cool, then stir in the Tia Maria.

To make the cupcakes, preheat the oven to 180°C (350°F/Gas 4). Place all the cupcake ingredients in a food processor and blend until smooth. Spoon tablespoons of the mixture into 24 patty cake tins or mini muffin tins and bake for 12 minutes. Cool on wire racks.

Make the filling by placing the sugar, egg yolks and Marsala in a bowl over a saucepan of simmering water and whisking until frothy. Remove and chill. Fold through the mascarpone. With a small knife, remove the lids from the cakes, cutting a well in the centre. Spoon a tablespoon of coffee syrup, then a tablespoon of the mascarpone, into the top of each cake. Replace the tops of the cakes and dust with cocoa powder. Allow to sit for several hours before serving.

chocolate creams makes 40 biscuits

155 g (5¹/₂ oz/1¹/₄ cups) plain
  (all-purpose) flour
2 tablespoons Dutch cocoa powder
1 teaspoon baking powder
100 g (3¹/₂ oz) unsalted butter
180 g (6 oz) dark chocolate
115 g (4 oz/¹/₂ cup) caster (superfine)
  sugar
2 eggs
unsweetened cocoa powder, extra,
`for dusting

chocolate cream
100 g (3¹/₂ oz) chocolate
2 tablespoons cream (whipping)

Sift together the flour, cocoa, baking powder and ³/₄ teaspoon of salt into a bowl. Melt the butter and chocolate in a bowl over a saucepan of simmering water, stirring until smooth. Remove from the heat. Add the sugar, stirring until dissolved. Stir in the eggs, one at a time, until well combined, then fold through the dry ingredients. Refrigerate the mixture for 20 minutes, or until just firm.

Make the chocolate cream by heating the chocolate and cream in a bowl over a saucepan of simmering water, stirring until smooth. Remove from the heat and allow to cool.

Preheat the oven to 180°C (350°F/ Gas 4). Pipe teaspoon-sized buttons onto baking trays lined with baking paper and bake for 5–7 minutes, or until firm. Cool slightly on the tray before transferring to a wire rack.

Stick the bases of the biscuits together with the chocolate cream and lightly dust with cocoa. Store in an airtight container.

fig surprise

makes 24

3 fresh figs
2 teaspoons finely chopped
  glacé ginger
2 tablespoons soft brown sugar
1/4 teaspoon grated lemon zest
1/4 teaspoon ground cinnamon
3 sheets filo pastry
50 g (1 3/4 oz) unsalted butter, melted
icing (confectioners') sugar, for dusting
vanilla or honey ice cream, to serve

Preheat the oven to 200°C (400°F/ Gas 6). Cut each fig into eight wedges. In a small bowl, combine the glacé ginger, brown sugar, lemon zest and cinnamon. Stir to combine. Cut each sheet of filo into eight equal pieces. Take one sheet and lightly brush it with the melted butter. Place a piece of fig against the side so that the stem end is outside the pastry. Place a little of the brown sugar mixture onto the fig. Fold the filo around the fig, leaving the stem section free. Repeat with the other pieces of pastry. Place the wrapped figs onto a baking tray lined with baking paper. Bake for 7–10 minutes, or until golden brown. Cool on a wire rack. Sprinkle with icing sugar and serve warm with vanilla or honey ice cream.

chocolate samosas   makes 24

1 egg yolk
12 wonton wrappers
125 g (4¹/2 oz) milk chocolate, finely
    chopped
70 g (2¹/2 oz/¹/2 cup) toasted hazelnuts,
    roughly chopped
2 sugar bananas, sliced
500 ml (17 fl oz/2 cups) vegetable oil
icing (confectioners') sugar, to serve
thick (double/heavy) cream, to serve

Whisk the egg yolk with 2 tablespoons of water in a bowl. Lay the wonton wrappers on a dry, clean surface and put some chocolate, hazelnuts and banana slices in the centre of each one. Brush the edges of the wonton wrappers with a little of the egg wash and twist the edges together. Put the wontons onto a dry plate, cover and refrigerate until needed.

Heat the oil in a deep-based frying pan or saucepan until it is beginning to shimmer. Put the wontons into the hot oil, a few at a time, and cook until golden. Remove and drain on paper towels. Repeat until all the wontons are cooked. Sprinkle with icing sugar and serve hot with a generous dollop of thick cream.

chocolate caramel 'brûlées'

serves 10

375 ml (13 fl oz/1½ cups) cream
  (whipping)
250 ml (9 fl oz/1 cup) milk
1 vanilla bean, split and scraped
5 egg yolks
165 g (5¾ oz/¾ cup) sugar
30 g (1 oz) dark chocolate, grated
Dutch cocoa powder, for dusting

Preheat the oven to 150°C (300°F/ Gas 2). Place the cream, milk and vanilla bean in a saucepan and heat until almost boiling. Remove from the heat.

In a bowl, beat the egg yolks with 55 g (2 oz/¼ cup) of the sugar and a pinch of salt until thick. Place the remaining sugar in a heavy-based saucepan. Melt it over medium heat. When it has become a golden colour, pour over the hot milk. Whisk until the toffeed sugar has dissolved. Pour this hot mixture over the egg mix. Whisk to combine. Strain and pour into ten 100 ml (3½ fl oz) ramekins. Place in a baking dish and fill the dish with hot water until the water comes two-thirds of the way up the side of the pots. Cover with foil and bake for 20–25 minutes. Remove from the oven and remove the foil.

Sprinkle the grated chocolate over the top of the custards until the surface is covered. Wipe the edges of the pots clean. Allow to cool. Serve sprinkled with cocoa powder.

strawberries with nutty filo

serves 4

30 g (1 oz/¹/₃ cup) flaked almonds
30 g (1 oz/¹/₄ cup) pistachio nuts
2 tablespoons honey
1 teaspoon grated lemon zest
1 tablespoon lemon juice
4 sheets filo pastry
40 g (1¹/₂ oz) unsalted butter, melted
1 teaspoon cinnamon
icing (confectioners') sugar
300 g (10¹/₂ oz/2 cups) strawberries,
   hulled and halved
cardamom and rosewater syrup
   (basics)

Preheat the oven to 180°C (350°F/ Gas 4). Finely chop the almonds and pistachios and put them in a small bowl along with the honey, lemon zest and juice. Put a piece of baking paper on a greased baking tray. Lay one of the filo sheets on top, brush the sheet with a little melted butter and then lay another sheet on top. Brush the top sheet with butter and sprinkle on the cinnamon and the nut mixture. Top with two more buttered sheets of pastry.

Bake the filo for 15 minutes, or until it is golden brown, then liberally cover the top with sifted icing sugar and break it into rough pieces.

Divide the strawberries among four plates. Top with the pastry. Drizzle with the cardamom and rosewater syrup.

chocolate brownies

makes 35 squares

125 g (4¹/2 oz) unsalted butter
125 g (4¹/2 oz) dark chocolate
4 eggs
300 g (10¹/2 oz) caster (superfine) sugar
125 g (4¹/2 oz/1 cup) plain (all-purpose) flour
30 g (1 oz/¹/4 cup) Dutch cocoa powder
1 teaspoon natural vanilla extract
60 g (2¹/4 oz/heaped ¹/2 cup) roughly ground hazelnuts
icing (confectioners') sugar or unsweetened cocoa powder, to serve

Preheat the oven to 180°C (350°F/ Gas 4). Melt the butter and chocolate in a medium-sized saucepan over low heat, stirring occasionally, until smooth. Allow to cool for 10 minutes. Beat the eggs and sugar in a large bowl until light and fluffy, then gradually add the cooled chocolate mix. Fold in the flour, cocoa powder, vanilla extract, hazelnuts and a pinch of salt. Pour into a greased 30 x 20 cm (12 x 8 in) baking tin lined with baking paper and bake for 30 minutes, or until the edges begin to pull away from the baking tin. Allow to cool in the tin. Cut into small squares and dust with icing sugar or unsweetened cocoa to serve.

figs in sauternes with crème fraîche parfait serves 6

12 fresh figs, quartered
400 ml (14 fl oz) sauternes
1 teaspoon honey

parfait
5 egg yolks
125 g (4½ oz/heaped ½ cup) caster
   (superfine) sugar
1 teaspoon natural vanilla extract
500 g (1 lb 2 oz/2 cups) crème fraîche

Put the figs in a bowl and cover with the sauterne. Drizzle with honey. Cover and refrigerate for 12 hours, or overnight.

Whisk the egg yolks, sugar and vanilla extract until the mixture is thick and very pale. Fold through the crème fraîche, then spoon into a 22 x 8 cm (8½ x 3¼ in) tin lined with baking paper. Freeze until firm. Slice the parfait into six thick slices and serve on chilled plates with the halved figs and a spoonful of the sauterne.

chocolate pudding   serves 6

60 g (2¼ oz/½ cup) unsweetened
  cocoa powder, plus extra
  for sprinkling
90 g (3¼ oz/½ cup) soft brown sugar
2 eggs
150 g (5½ oz/⅔ cup) caster
  (superfine) sugar
50 g (1¾ oz) unsalted butter, chopped
100 g (3½ oz/⅔ cup) chopped
  dark chocolate
125 ml (4 fl oz/½ cup) milk
125 g (4½ oz/1 cup) sifted self-raising
  flour
cream or custard, to serve

Preheat the oven to 180°C (350°F/ Gas 4). Butter six 300 ml (10½ fl oz) ramekins. Put 40 g (1½ oz/⅓ cup) cocoa powder, the brown sugar and 300 ml (10½ fl oz) of boiling water in a large pitcher.

Put the eggs and caster sugar in a large bowl and lightly beat together.

Put the butter, chocolate and milk in a small saucepan over medium heat for 3 minutes, or until the butter and chocolate have melted. Remove from the heat and cool slightly.

Add the self-raising flour and remaining cocoa powder to the beaten egg mixture and then stir in the melted chocolate. Divide the batter among the ramekins and spoon the hot water mixture over the puddings. Transfer to a baking tray and bake for 30 minutes, or until firm. Dust with cocoa and serve with cream or warm custard.

chocolate nut meringues
with cream and berries serves 6

3 egg whites
200 g (7 oz) caster (superfine) sugar
2 tablespoons dark cocoa powder
2 tablespoons ground hazelnuts
50 g (1³/₄ oz) flaked almonds
150 ml (5 fl oz) cream (whipping)
500 g (1 lb 2 oz) mixed berries

Preheat the oven to 150°C (300°F/ Gas 2). Line a large baking tray with baking paper. Whisk the egg whites until they form soft peaks and then slowly add the sugar, continuing to beat until the mixture is white and glossy. Fold in the cocoa and ground hazelnuts, then spoon the meringue into six large dollops on the tray. Using the back of the spoon, create a dip in the top of each meringue. Sprinkle with the almonds and bake for 45 minutes. Turn off the heat, but leave the meringues to cool in the oven with the door ajar. Store in an airtight container until ready to use. Serve topped with whipped cream and berries.

rich chocolate cake   serves 10

250 g (9 oz) unsalted butter
200 g (7 oz) dark chocolate
375 ml (13 fl oz/1½ cups) strong coffee
450 g (1 lb/2 cups) caster (superfine) sugar
175 g (6 oz/1½ cups) plain (all-purpose) flour
1 teaspoon baking powder
30 g (1 oz/¼ cup) unsweetened cocoa powder
2 eggs
2 teaspoons natural vanilla extract
1 quantity chocolate icing (basics)
whipped cream or vanilla ice cream, to serve

Preheat the oven to 180°C (350°F/ Gas 4). Grease and line a 25 cm (10 in) springform tin. Put the butter, chocolate and coffee in a saucepan over low heat and cook until the chocolate has melted. Add the sugar and stir to dissolve. Remove from the heat and pour into a bowl. Whisk in the dry ingredients, then add the eggs and vanilla. Whisk to combine.

Pour the batter into the prepared tin and bake for 1 hour. Allow the cake to cool in the tin before removing. Cover with chocolate icing. Serve with whipped cream or vanilla ice cream.

chocolate marquise serves 4-6

100 g (3¹/2 oz) dark chocolate
50 g (1³/4 oz) unsalted butter, softened
50 g (1³/4 oz) caster (superfine) sugar
2 tablespoons unsweetened cocoa
   powder
2 egg yolks
1 teaspoon rosewater
150 ml (5 fl oz) cream (whipping)
150 g (5¹/2 oz) raspberries, to serve
6 white nectarines, sliced, to serve
45 g (1¹/2 oz/¹/2 cup) flaked almonds,
   toasted, to serve
icing (confectioners') sugar, for dusting

Melt the chocolate in a heatproof bowl set over a saucepan of boiling water, making sure the base does not touch the water. Beat the butter with half the sugar until pale and fluffy. Mix in the cocoa. Beat the yolks with the remaining sugar until pale and smooth, then add the rosewater. Whip the cream until thick.

Mix the melted chocolate into the butter mixture, fold in the egg mixture, then fold in the cream. Spoon into a lined 22 x 8 cm (8¹/2 x 3¹/4 in) tin and chill for 3 hours, or until set.

Turn out the marquise and cut into thick slices. Serve with raspberries, white nectarines, toasted flaked almonds and a dusting of icing sugar.

strawberry rice pudding

makes 10 small bowls, or 6 regular serves

500 ml (17 fl oz/2 cups) milk
55 g (2 oz/1/4 cup) sugar
2 teaspoons finely chopped orange
   zest
3 cardamom pods
75 g (21/2 oz/1/3 cup) short-grain rice
125 g (41/2 oz/1/2 cup) cream, whipped
60 g (21/4 oz/scant 1/2 cup) chopped
   pistachios
300 g (101/2 oz/2 cups) strawberries
icing (confectioners') sugar, for dusting

Bring the milk to the boil with the sugar, orange zest, cardamom pods and a pinch of salt, then tip in the rice. Reduce the heat and simmer gently for 30 minutes, or until the rice is cooked. Remove the cardamom pods. Allow the rice to cool, then fold in the cream with half of the pistachios. Layer the rice and strawberries into small bowls, starting with the rice, then fruit, and so on. Top with a sprinkle of the remaining pistachios and dust with icing sugar.

mini chocolate cakes   makes 12

125 g (4¹/₂ oz) unsalted butter
100 g (3¹/₂ oz) dark chocolate
185 ml (6 fl oz/³/₄ cup) strong coffee
250 g (9 oz/1 cup) sugar
1 egg
1 teaspoon natural vanilla extract
80 g (2³/₄ oz/³/₄ cup) plain (all-purpose) flour
1 teaspoon baking powder
30 g (1 oz/¹/₄ cup) unsweetened cocoa powder
1 quantity chocolate icing (basics)
whipped cream or vanilla ice cream, to serve

Preheat the oven to 180°C (350°F/ Gas 4). Put the butter, chocolate and coffee in a saucepan over low heat and leave it until the chocolate has melted. Add the sugar, stirring until it has dissolved, then pour the chocolate mixture into a bowl. Whisk in the egg and vanilla before sifting in the dry ingredients. Stir together.

Spoon the mixture into 12 patty cake tins or muffin holes lined with cases and bake for 15 minutes. Allow the cakes to cool before removing them. Ice the cakes and serve with whipped cream or vanilla ice cream.

chocolate and hazelnut slice

makes 20 pieces

250 g (9 oz) unsalted butter
325 g (11¹/₂ oz/1¹/₂ cups) sugar
90 g (3¹/₄ oz/³/₄ cup) unsweetened
  cocoa powder
40 g (1¹/₂ oz/¹/₃ cup) plain (all-purpose)
  flour
¹/₂ teaspoon baking powder
4 eggs
125 g (4¹/₂ oz/1 cup) chopped toasted
  hazelnuts
200 g (7 oz/1¹/₃ cups) chopped
  chocolate or chocolate chips
unsweetened cocoa powder, extra,
  for dusting

Preheat the oven to 180°C (350°F/ Gas 4). Grease and line a 23 cm (9 in) square cake tin. Melt the butter with the sugar in a saucepan over low heat. When the butter has melted, stir to ensure that the sugar has dissolved. Remove the pan from the heat. Sift the cocoa powder, flour and baking powder into a large bowl and add a pinch of salt. Make a well in the centre and stir in the melted butter and sugar, then stir in the eggs. Add the hazelnuts and chocolate. Lightly stir to combine, then pour into the prepared tin. Bake for 25–30 minutes. Remove from the oven and cool in the pan. Cut into pieces and dust with cocoa.

summer berries with crème anglaise
serves 6-8

250 ml (9 fl oz/1 cup) milk
250 ml (9 fl oz/1 cup) cream (whipping)
1 vanilla bean
5 egg yolks
80 g (2³/₄ oz/¹/₃ cup) caster (superfine)
  sugar
500 g (1 lb 2 oz) mixed raspberries,
  blackberries and blueberries

Put the milk and cream into a heavy-based saucepan. Lightly rub the vanilla bean between your fingers to soften it. With the point of a small sharp knife, cut the bean in half lengthways and put it into the saucepan. Heat the saucepan over medium heat and bring the milk and cream just to simmering point. Remove the saucepan from the heat.

Whisk the egg yolks with the sugar in a bowl until light and foamy. Whisk a little of the warm milk and cream into the eggs. Add the remaining liquid, reserving the vanilla bean. Whisk to combine. Rinse the saucepan and return the mixture to the saucepan.

Cook over medium heat, stirring constantly with a wooden spoon, until the mixture thickens and coats the back of the spoon. Strain into a bowl. Scrape the vanilla seeds from the split bean into the custard. Stir the specks of vanilla through the custard. Pour into a serving pitcher. Serve with the mixed berries.

butterfly cakes

175 g (6 oz) unsalted butter, softened
175 g (6 oz/3/4 cup) caster (superfine)
  sugar
3 eggs
125 ml (4 fl oz/1/2 cup) milk
1 teaspoon natural vanilla extract
175 g (6 oz/11/2 cups) self-raising flour,
  sifted
250 ml (9 fl oz/1 cup) cream (whipping)
6 strawberries, quartered
icing (confectioners') sugar, for dusting

Preheat the oven to 180°C (350°F/ Gas 4). Line a 12 patty cake tins with cases. Beat the butter with the caster sugar in a mixing bowl until pale and creamy. Add the eggs, milk and vanilla extract. Stir to combine, then fold in the self-raising flour. Spoon the batter into the patty cases and bake for 15–20 minutes, or until golden and firm. Transfer the cupcakes to a wire rack to cool.

Cut shallow rounds from the centre of each cake using the point of a sharp knife, then cut in half. Spoon a dollop of the whipped cream into each cavity and position two halves of the cake tops in the cream to resemble butterfly wings. Top with the quartered strawberries. Dust with icing sugar.

hazelnut meringue with berries

2 egg whites
115 g (1/2 cup) caster (superfine) sugar
35 g (11/4 oz/1/3 cup) ground hazelnuts
310 ml (11/4 cups) cream (whipping)
1 teaspoon natural vanilla extract
450 g (1 lb) mixed raspberries,
   blackberries, blueberries and
   strawberries cut into smaller pieces

Preheat the oven to 150°C (300°F/ Gas 2). Whisk the egg whites until they form soft peaks and then slowly add the sugar, continuing to beat until the mixture is stiff. Fold in the hazelnuts.

Line two baking trays with baking paper and divide the meringue between them, putting a big dollop in the middle of each tray. Using the back of a spoon, spread the mixture out until you have two 20 cm (8 in) circles of meringue.

Bake for 40 minutes. Turn the oven off, but leave the meringues in the oven, with the door ajar, for 30 minutes.

Whip the cream and fold in the vanilla extract. When the meringues are cool, put one of the rounds on a serving plate. Top with some of the cream and half the berries, arranging them so that they make a flat surface for the next meringue layer. Put the other meringue on top and decorate with the cream and remaining berries. Allow to sit for 15 minutes before serving.

mini danish

1 sheet ready-prepared puff pastry
1 egg
3 tablespoons milk
4 small plums, cut into eight wedges

pastry cream
50 g (1 3/4 oz) caster (superfine) sugar
2 egg yolks
25 g (3/4 oz) cornflour (cornstarch)
1 vanilla bean
250 ml (9 fl oz/1 cup) milk
25 g (3/4 oz) unsalted butter
icing (confectioners') sugar, for dusting

To make the pastry cream, whisk the sugar, egg yolks and cornflour in a bowl. Split open the vanilla bean. Place it in a saucepan with the milk. Slowly bring to the boil then remove from the heat. Whisk 80 ml (2 1/2 fl oz/ 1/3 cup) of the hot milk into the egg mixture. Tip this mixture into the saucepan containing the remainder of the milk, and whisk. Return the pan to the heat. Bring back to the boil, stirring. Boil for 1 minute. Pass through a sieve into a bowl. Discard the vanilla bean. Add the butter and stir until melted. Allow the pastry cream to cool. Cover with plastic wrap and refrigerate.

Preheat the oven to 180°C (350°F/ Gas 4). Cut the sheet of pastry into 16 small squares. Beat the egg and milk together and set aside. Place each of the squares into a shallow patty cake tin or muffin hole. Prick the bases with a fork and fill with a teaspoon of pastry cream. Top with sliced plums. Fold the pastry over the fruit to enclose it, then glaze with the egg wash. Bake for 12 minutes, or until golden. Serve warm or at room temperature. Dust with icing sugar.

coconut, raspberry and white chocolate slice makes 20 pieces

125 g (4¹/2 oz) unsalted butter
150 g (5¹/2 oz) white chocolate
175 g (6 oz/³/4 cup) caster (superfine) sugar
125 g (4¹/2 oz/1 cup) self-raising flour
90 g (3¹/4 oz/1 cup) desiccated coconut
2 eggs, beaten
150 g (5¹/2 oz/1¹/4 cups) fresh raspberries
icing (confectioners') sugar, for dusting

Preheat the oven to 180°C (350°F/ Gas 4). Grease and line a 26 x 16 cm (10¹/2 x 6¹/4 in) slice tin. Melt the butter and white chocolate in a saucepan over low heat. Add the caster sugar and stir to combine. Pour into a large bowl and add the self-raising flour and desiccated coconut. Stir to combine, then add the eggs. Stir lightly to just combine, then fold in the raspberries. Pour the mixture into the prepared tin and bake for 40 minutes, or until firm. Cool in the tin. Cut into 20 pieces and dust with icing sugar.

chocolate chip cookies makes 20

125 g (4 1/2 oz) unsalted butter, softened
175 g (6 oz/1 cup) soft brown sugar
1 teaspoon natural vanilla extract
1 tablespoon milk
1 egg, beaten
175 g (6 oz/1 1/2 cups) plain
  (all-purpose) flour, sifted
1 teaspoon baking powder, sifted
275 g (9 3/4 oz/1 1/2 cups) dark
  chocolate chips

Preheat the oven to 180°C (350°F/ Gas 4). Grease and line a baking tray with baking paper. Beat the butter with the brown sugar in a bowl until light and creamy. Add the vanilla extract, milk and egg and work them lightly into the butter mixture. Gently fold in the flour and baking powder. Stir in the chocolate chips. Drop heaped tablespoons of the mixture onto a baking tray, leaving about 3 cm (1 1/4 in) between each cookie. Bake for 15 minutes, or until lightly golden. Transfer the cookies to a wire rack to cool. Store in an airtight container.

raspberry ripple cake serves 10

300 g (10¹/2 oz/2 cups) frozen
  raspberries
250 g (9 oz/2 cups) plain (all-purpose)
  flour
2 teaspoons baking powder
¹/4 teaspoon salt
125 g (4¹/2 oz) unsalted butter, softened
225 g (8 oz/1 cup) caster (superfine)
  sugar
3 eggs, lightly beaten
250 g (9 oz/1 cup) sour cream
20 g (³/4 oz) butter, melted
125 g (4¹/2 oz/1 cup) icing
  (confectioners') sugar, sifted

Preheat the oven to 180°C (350°F/ Gas 4). Grease and line a 23 cm (9 in) springform tin. Put the frozen raspberries into a bowl and lightly crush them. Reserve 1 tablespoon of their juice in another bowl to make the icing.

Sift the flour, baking powder and salt into a large bowl. Cream the butter and sugar until pale and fluffy, then stir in the eggs. Add the dry ingredients, alternating with the sour cream, and mixing well after each addition. Spoon one-third of the batter into the prepared tin, then spoon over half the raspberries. Repeat with another third of the batter and the remaining raspberries. Top with the remaining batter. Bake for 50 minutes, or until a skewer comes out clean. Allow the cake to cool in the tin before turning out and icing it.

To make the icing, add the melted butter to the reserved raspberry juice. Slowly stir in the sifted icing sugar until the icing has a smooth runny consistency. Spoon over the cake.

fig and burnt butter tart

serves 8

6 fresh figs
1 pre-baked shortcrust tart case (basics)
3 eggs
170 g (3/4 cup) caster (superfine) sugar
30 g (1 oz/1/4 cup) plain (all-purpose)
   flour
185 g (61/2 oz) unsalted butter

Preheat the oven to 180°C (350°F/ Gas 4). Slice the figs into quarters and arrange them in the tart case with the narrow ends pointing up. Beat the eggs and sugar until they are pale and fluffy, then fold in the flour. Heat the butter in a saucepan over high heat and when it begins to froth and turn light brown, pour the hot butter into the egg mixture and continue to beat for a minute. Pour the filling over the figs and bake for 25 minutes, or until the filling is cooked and golden brown. Allow to cool before serving.

chocolate ice cream   serves 4

375 ml (13 fl oz/1¹/₂ cups) milk
250 ml (9 fl oz/1 cup) cream (whipping)
100 g (3¹/₂ oz/²/₃ cup) roughly chopped
  dark chocolate
4 egg yolks
40 g (1¹/₂ oz/¹/₃ cup) caster (superfine)
  sugar
2 tablespoons unsweetened cocoa
  powder

Put the milk, cream and chocolate in a heavy-based saucepan over medium heat. Bring the milk and cream just to simmering point, stirring to help the chocolate to melt. Remove the saucepan from the heat.

Put the egg yolks and sugar in a mixing bowl and whisk until light and foamy. Add the cocoa powder and whisk again. Whisk in a little of the warm chocolate mixture, then add the remaining liquid and whisk to combine. Return the mixture to the cleaned saucepan. Cook over medium heat, stirring constantly with a wooden spoon, until the mixture thickens and coats the back of the spoon. Strain into a bowl and allow to cool. Churn in an ice-cream machine according to the manufacturer's instructions.

bloody mary whisky sour rose petal sherbert sangria watermelon and chilli cooler bellini strawberry lassi cosmopolitan brandy alexander campari classic champagne cocktail sour cherry blossom watermelon, mint and vodka rhubarb, strawberry and white rum chiller mexican shot ripe cherry whisky sour rose petal sherbert sorbet vodka shot bloody mary brandy alexander strawberry lassi cosmopolitan ripe cherry

05   drinks

rhubarb, strawberry and white rum chiller watermelon and chilli cooler bellini champagne cocktail sour cherry blossom sangria watermelon, mint and vodka mexican shot bloody mary campari classic rose petal sherbert brandy alexander strawberry lassi champagne

bloody mary

150 g (5^{1}/$_{2}$ oz) tomatoes, finely
   chopped
80 ml (2^{1}/$_{2}$ fl oz/^{1}/$_{3}$ cup) tomato juice
60 ml (2 fl oz/^{1}/$_{4}$ cup) vodka
^{1}/$_{4}$ teaspoon Worcestershire sauce
^{1}/$_{4}$ teaspoon Tabasco sauce
1 teaspoon horseradish cream
1 teaspoon lime juice
ice cubes, to serve
celery, lime and freshly ground black
   pepper, to garnish

Put the tomatoes and ^{1}/$_{4}$ teaspoon of salt in a bowl and allow to sit for 30 minutes. Put the tomato pieces in a blender with the tomato juice and blend until smooth. Put the tomato juice into a shaker with the vodka, Worcestershire sauce, Tabasco sauce, horseradish cream and lime juice and shake vigorously. Pour over ice and garnish with a celery stalk, a round of lime and freshly ground black pepper.

strawberry lassi   serves 2

150 g (5¹/2 oz/1 cup) hulled strawberries
250 g (9 oz/1 cup) Greek-style yoghurt
1 teaspoon honey
8 ice cubes

Combine the strawberries, yoghurt, honey and ice cubes in a blender. Blend until smooth and pour into chilled glasses.

ripe cherry

60 ml (2 fl oz/¼ cup) **Framboise**
30 ml (1 fl oz) **Malibu**
30 ml (1 fl oz) **white crème de cacao**
crushed ice, to serve

Put all the ingredients except the ice in a cocktail shaker and shake well. Pour over the crushed ice and serve immediately.

watermelon and chilli cooler

serves 2

chilli syrup
2 large red chillies
110 g (3³/4 oz/1/2 cup) sugar

500 ml (17 fl oz/2 cups) watermelon juice
2 tablespoons lime juice
mint sprigs, to garnish
ice cubes, to serve

To make the chilli syrup, put the chillies, sugar and 125 ml (4 fl oz/ 1/2 cup) of water in a small saucepan and bring to the boil. Reduce the heat and simmer for 5 minutes. Remove the chillies. Cool the syrup. Place in a jar or bottle. Store in the refrigerator until ready to use.

Blend together the watermelon juice, 2 tablespoons of the chilli syrup and the lime juice. Pour into glasses filled with ice cubes, and garnish with sprigs of mint.

rose petal sherbet   serves 8

4 red organic roses, petals removed
220 g (7³/₄ oz/1 cup) sugar
1 tablespoon rosewater
2 litres (70 fl oz/8 cups) sparkling
   mineral water

Put the rose petals, sugar and 310 ml (10³/₄ fl oz/1¹/₄ cups) of water in a large saucepan and bring to the boil. Reduce the heat and simmer for 8 minutes, or until a light syrup has been made. Remove any scum as it forms. Cool and stir in the rosewater. To serve, pour the syrup into chilled glasses and top with sparkling mineral water.

sangria

a bottle of Rioja or a light red wine
100 ml (3 1/2 fl oz) sugar syrup
60 ml (2 fl oz/1/4 cup) Cointreau
60 ml (2 fl oz/1/4 cup) lemon juice
1 orange, thinly sliced
1 lime, thinly sliced
ice cubes, to serve

In a large pitcher, put the Rioja, sugar syrup, Cointreau, lemon juice, orange and lime. Stir all the ingredients well and top with ice.

sorbet vodka shot   serves 6

6 tablespoons fruit sorbet
125 ml (4 fl oz/1/2 cup) vodka

Divide the fruit sorbet between six chilled shot glasses and pour a tablespoon of vodka over each.

mexican shot

90 ml (3 fl oz) tequila

90 ml (3 fl oz) tomato juice

200 g (7 oz/1 cup) roma (plum)
   tomatoes, roughly chopped

1 teaspoon lime juice

1 roma (plum) tomato, extra, finely
   diced

2 tablespoons finely chopped
   coriander (cilantro) leaves

chilli syrup

2 large red chillies

110 g (3³/4 oz/¹/2 cup) sugar

To make the chilli syrup, put the chillies, sugar and 125 ml (4 fl oz/ ¹/2 cup) of water in a small saucepan. Bring to the boil. Reduce the heat and simmer for 5 minutes. Remove the chillies. Cool the syrup and place in a jar or bottle. Store in the refrigerator until ready to use.

Put the tequila, tomato juice, chopped tomatoes, 1 tablespoon of the chilli syrup and the lime juice in a blender and blend until smooth. Pour into a small container and fold in the diced tomato and coriander. Place in the freezer for several hours or overnight. Break up with a fork, or place in a blender and pulse. Spoon into cocktail glasses and serve immediately.

rhubarb, strawberry and white rum chiller

serves 2

6 strawberries
60 ml (2 fl oz/1/4 cup) white rum
1 teaspoon natural vanilla extract
8 ice cubes

stewed rhubarb

300 g (10 1/2 oz) rhubarb (approximately
   7 stems)
55 g (2 oz/1/4 cup) caster (superfine)
   sugar

To make the stewed rhubarb, trim the rhubarb stems and cut them into four pieces. Put the rhubarb, sugar and 60 ml (2 fl oz/1/4 cup) of water in a stainless steel saucepan over medium heat. Cover and simmer for 10 minutes. Remove from heat and allow to cool.

Put the stewed rhubarb, strawberries, white rum, vanilla extract and ice cubes in a blender and blend until smooth. Pour into chilled glasses.

cosmopolitan

ice cubes
60 ml (2 fl oz/1/4 cup) vodka
30 ml (1 fl oz) Cointreau
1 teaspoon lime juice
30 ml (1 fl oz) cranberry juice

Fill a cocktail shaker with ice cubes and add the vodka, Cointreau, lime juice and cranberry juice. Shake vigorously, then strain into a chilled cocktail glass.

champagne cocktail

1 sugar cube
3 dashes Angostura bitters
3 teaspoons brandy
Champagne

Moisten the sugar cube with the bitters and put in a champagne flute. Pour in the brandy and top with Champagne.

watermelon, mint and vodka

serves 1

2 sprigs mint
5 watermelon juice ice cubes
125 ml (4 fl oz/$^1/_2$ cup) watermelon
  juice
$^1/_2$ teaspoon lime juice
30 ml (1 fl oz) vodka

Put the mint sprigs and the watermelon ice cubes in a tall glass and pour over the watermelon juice, lime juice and vodka. Stir well.

sour cherry blossom   serves 2

ice cubes
1 tablespoon cream (whipping)
60 ml (2 fl oz/1/4 cup) gin
60 ml (2 fl oz/1/4 cup) sour cherry nectar
1 egg white
1 tablespoon Framboise

Into a shaker half-filled with ice cubes, put the cream, gin, sour cherry nectar, egg white and framboise. Shake vigorously and pour into small, chilled cocktail glasses.

campari classic

125 ml (4 fl oz/1/2 cup) orange juice
60 ml (2 fl oz/1/4 cup) Campari
6 ice cubes
sliced orange, to garnish

Pour the orange juice and Campari into a tall glass and top with the ice cubes. Garnish with sliced orange.

whisky sour

ice cubes
60 ml (2 fl oz/¼ cup) whisky
30 ml (1 fl oz) lemon juice
1 teaspoon caster (superfine) sugar
1 egg white
ice cubes, to serve
1 maraschino cherry, to serve

Three-quarters fill a cocktail shaker with ice cubes. Add the whisky, lemon juice, sugar and a dash of egg white. Shake well. Strain into a small cocktail glass containing ice cubes and a maraschino cherry.

brandy alexander   serves 1

50 ml (1³/₄ fl oz) brandy
30 ml (1 fl oz) crème de cacao
1 tablespoon cream (whipping)
3–4 ice cubes
sprinkle of nutmeg, to garnish

Put the brandy, crème de cacao, cream and ice cubes in a cocktail shaker and shake vigorously several times. Pour into a cocktail glass and garnish with a sprinkle of nutmeg.

roasted tomato pasta sauce mushroom pasta sauce
home-made pasta pesto polenta home-made pizza dough
home-made focaccia vegetable stock chicken stock
veal stock fish stock roasted chicken roast lamb
roast beef olive and basil stuffing for lamb roasted
sweet potato horseradish gremolata beef marinade
lamb marinade caponata rouille chilli-lime sauce red
wine sauce shortcrust tart case shortcrust tartlets

06 basics

chocolate icing cardamom and rosewater syrup roasted
tomato pasta sauce mushroom pasta sauce home-made
pasta pesto polenta home-made pizza dough basics
home-made focaccia vegetable stock chicken stock
veal stock fish stock roasted chicken roast lamb

roasted tomato pasta sauce

serves 4

6 roma (plum) tomatoes
10 basil leaves
1 garlic clove
2 tablespoons extra virgin olive oil
1 teaspoon balsamic vinegar
1 teaspoon sugar

Preheat the oven to 200°C (400°F/ Gas 6). Put the tomatoes on a baking tray and roast until the skins are beginning to blacken all over. Put the whole tomatoes, including the charred skin and any juices, into a food processor or blender with the basil, garlic, oil, balsamic vinegar and sugar. Blend to form a thick sauce, thinning the mixture with a little warm water if necessary.

Toss the sauce through warm pasta and serve with grated parmesan cheese and a few basil leaves.

mushroom pasta sauce serves 4

2 tablespoons butter
1 crushed garlic clove
400 g (14 oz) halved button
  mushrooms
2 large roughly chopped
  field mushrooms
1 teaspoon thyme leaves
4 tablespoons white wine

Heat the butter in a large frying pan over medium heat and add the garlic, and mushrooms. Sauté for 5 minutes, then add the thyme leaves and white wine. Simmer for a further 1 minute. Toss the sauce through warm pasta and drizzle with oil. Add the parmesan cheese and toss to combine.

home-made pasta

makes enough pasta for 4 main servings

400 g (14 oz/3¹/4 cups) plain
   (all-purpose) flour
¹/2 **teaspoon salt**
4 eggs
50 g (1³/4 oz/heaped ¹/3 cup)
   semolina flour

Put the plain flour into a food processor with the salt. Add the eggs and process until the mixture begins to come together in a rough dough.

Put the dough on a lightly floured board and dust with the semolina flour. Knead until the dough is smooth. Divide the dough into four equal portions and wrap in plastic wrap. Refrigerate for 30 minutes.

Put the pasta dough through a pasta machine according to the manufacturer's instructions. When it has reached the desired thickness and cut, set it on a clean tray liberally sprinkled with more semolina flour or plain (all-purpose) flour. Toss the pasta through your fingers to separate it, then lay it on a floured tray while you cut the remaining dough.

pesto

150 g (5¹/2 oz) basil, leaves removed
140 g (5 oz) flat-leaf (Italian) parsley,
  roughly chopped
100 g (3¹/2 oz/1 cup) grated parmesan
  cheese
1 garlic clove
80 g (2³/4 oz/¹/2 cup) pine nuts, toasted
170 ml (5¹/2 fl oz/²/3 cup) olive oil

Put the basil, parsley, parmesan, garlic and pine nuts into a food processor or a pestle and mortar and blend or pound the mixture to make a thick paste.

Add the oil in a steady stream until the paste has a spoonable consistency.

If you want to keep your pesto, put it in a sterilized jar and add a layer of olive oil on top. This will prevent the surface of the pesto oxidizing and turning brown. Keep the pesto in the fridge for up to 2 weeks.

polenta

350 g (12 oz/2¹/₃ cups) polenta
100 g (3¹/₂ oz) butter, cut into cubes
100 g (3¹/₂ oz1 cup) grated parmesan cheese

Bring 2 litres (70 fl oz/8 cups) of water and a teaspoon of sea salt to the boil in a large saucepan. Lower the heat to a simmer and slowly add the polenta in a steady stream, stirring with a whisk to blend it smoothly. Reduce the heat to low and, stirring occasionally, allow the polenta to cook for 30 minutes. The polenta is cooked when it begins to pull away from the sides of the saucepan. Stir in the butter and parmesan. Season with sea salt and freshly ground black pepper and serve immediately.

home-made pizza dough

makes 1 quantity pizza dough or 2 medium pizza
bases, approximately 23 cm (9 in) in diameter
depending on the preferred thickness

2 teaspoons dried yeast or 15 g (1/2 oz)
  fresh yeast
1 teaspoon sugar
250 g (9 oz/2 cups) plain (all-purpose)
  flour
1 egg
21/2 tablespoons milk
1 teaspoon sea salt

Put the yeast into a small bowl with the sugar and 4 tablespoons warm water. Lightly stir to combine. Set aside for 10–15 minutes, or until the mixture starts to froth. Sift the flour into a bowl and make a well in the centre. Add the egg, milk, sea salt and the yeast mixture. Gradually work the ingredients together to form a stiff dough.

Turn the dough out onto a floured surface and knead until smooth and elastic. Oil a large bowl with a little olive oil and put the dough in it. Rub a little oil over the dough before covering it with a damp cloth. Put the bowl in a warm place for 2 hours until the dough has doubled in size.

Preheat the oven to 200°C (400°F/ Gas 6). Divide the dough in half and roll it out on a floured surface. Put the dough onto two oiled baking trays and add your toppings. Bake for 15 minutes.

home-made focaccia

450 g (1 lb/3²/₃ cups) plain
(all-purpose) flour

pinch of sea salt

2 teaspoons dried yeast or 15 g (¹/₂ oz)
fresh yeast

1 teaspoon sugar

3 tablespoons olive oil

2 tablespoons extra virgin olive oil

1 tablespoon sea salt, for sprinkling

Put the plain (all-purpose) flour into a large bowl with a good pinch of sea salt. Put the yeast in a small bowl with 250 ml (9 fl oz/1 cup) warm water and the sugar. Set aside for 10 minutes. When the mixture has started to froth, add it to the flour along with the oil. Work the ingredients together to form a rough dough before turning out onto a floured board.

Knead the dough until it is smooth and elastic. Put into an oiled bowl and cover with a tea towel. Leave the bowl in a warm place for 1 hour until the dough has doubled in size.

Preheat the oven to 200°C (400°F/ Gas 6). Put the dough onto an oiled 34 x 24 cm (13¹/₂ x 9¹/₂ in) baking tray and press it out until it covers the tray. Use your fingers to make dimples in the dough and then drizzle with 2 tablespoons extra virgin olive oil and sprinkle with the sea salt. Allow to rise for a further 20 minutes. Bake for 20 minutes, or until the focaccia is cooked through and golden brown on top.

vegetable stock

makes about 2 litres (70 fl oz/8 cups)

2 tablespoons unsalted butter
2 garlic cloves, crushed
2 onions, roughly chopped
4 leeks, coarsely chopped
3 carrots, coarsely chopped
3 celery stalks, thickly sliced
1 fennel bulb, coarsely chopped
1 handful flat-leaf (Italian) parsley
2 sprigs of thyme
2 black peppercorns

Put the butter, garlic and onions into a large, heavy-based saucepan. Put the pan over medium heat and stir until the onion is soft and transparent. Add the leeks, carrots, celery stalks, fennel bulb, parsley, thyme and peppercorns. Add 4 litres (140 fl oz/ 16 cups) water and bring to the boil. Reduce the heat and simmer for 2 hours. Allow to cool. Strain into another saucepan, using the back of a large spoon to press the liquid from the vegetables. Bring the stock to the boil, then reduce the heat to a rolling boil until the stock is reduced by half.

chicken stock

makes about 2 litres (70 fl oz/8 cups)

1 whole fresh chicken
1 onion, sliced
2 celery stalks, sliced
1 leek, roughly chopped
1 bay leaf
a few flat-leaf (Italian) parsley stalks
6 peppercorns

Fill a large heavy-based saucepan with 3 litres (105 fl oz/12 cups) cold water. Cut a fresh chicken into several large pieces and put them into the pan.

Bring just to the boil, then reduce the heat to a simmer. Skim any fat from the surface, then add the onion, celery stalks, leek, bay leaf, parsley stalks and peppercorns. Maintain the heat at a low simmer for 2 hours.

Strain the stock into a bowl and allow to cool. Using a large spoon, remove any fat that has risen to the surface. If a more concentrated flavour is required, return the stock to a saucepan and simmer over low heat. If you are not using the stock immediately, cover and refrigerate or freeze it.

veal stock

makes about 2 litres (70 fl oz/8 cups)

1 kg (2 lb 4 oz) veal bones
2 tablespoons olive oil
2 chopped onions
3 garlic cloves
2 roughly chopped leeks
2 sliced celery stalks
2 roughly chopped large tomatoes
1 bay leaf
6 black peppercorns

Preheat the oven to 200°C (400°F/ Gas 6). Put the veal bones and olive oil into a large roasting tin, rub the oil over the bones and bake for 30 minutes. Add the onions, garlic, leeks, celery stalks and tomatoes to the tin. Continue baking for about 1 hour, or until the bones are well browned. Transfer the roasted bones and vegetables to a large heavy-based saucepan and cover with plenty of cold water. Bring to the boil over medium heat, then reduce the heat to a simmer. Skim any fat from the surface, then add the bay leaf and black peppercorns. Cook at a low simmer for 4 hours. Strain the stock into a bowl and allow to cool. Using a large spoon, remove any fat on the surface. Return the stock to a saucepan and simmer over low heat to reduce and concentrate the flavour.

fish stock

makes about 1 litre (35 fl oz/4 cups)

1 kg (2 lb 4 oz) fish bones
1 chopped onion,
1 chopped carrot
1 sliced fennel bulb
2 sliced celery stalks
a few sprigs of thyme
a few parsley sprigs
4 black peppercorns

Put the fish bones into a large saucepan with 2 litres (70 fl oz/ 8 cups) water. Bring just to the boil, then reduce the heat and simmer for 20 minutes. Strain the liquid through a fine sieve into another saucepan to remove the bones and then add the onion, carrot, fennel, celery, thyme, parsley and peppercorns. Bring back to the boil, then reduce the heat and simmer for a further 35 minutes. Strain into a bowl and allow to cool.

olive and basil stuffing
for lamb

85 g (3 oz/^{1}/2 cup) pitted kalamata
  olives
15 basil leaves
1 handful flat-leaf (Italian) parsley
  leaves
2 garlic cloves
100 g (3^1/2 oz/1 cup) ground almonds

Put the olives, basil leaves, parsley leaves, garlic and ground almonds into a food processor. Pulse once or twice to form a rough paste. Press the paste into a boned leg of lamb and use a skewer to keep the opening closed. Roast the lamb immediately.

bellini

1/2 ripe white peach
1 teaspoon caster (superfine) sugar
Champagne

Purée the peach and sugar and set aside. Pour a little Champagne into two champagne flutes and divide the peach purée between the glasses. Lightly stir. Top up with Champagne.

roasted sweet potato   serves 4

2 large orange sweet potatoes
1 tablespoon oil

Preheat the oven to 180°C (350°F/ Gas 4). Peel the sweet potatoes and cut them into chunks. Toss the potatoes in the oil. Season with a good sprinkling of sea salt and some freshly ground black pepper.

Spread the potatoes out on a baking tray in a single layer. Roast them for 30 minutes, or until they are browned and cooked through.

horseradish gremolata serves 4

3 tablespoons finely chopped flat-leaf
   (Italian) parsley
1 tablespoon finely grated lemon zest
1 tablespoon finely grated fresh
   horseradish root

Mix all the ingredients together in a bowl. Serve scattered over osso bucco or seared lamb backstrap just before serving.

beef marinade

250 ml (9 fl oz/1 cup) red wine
2 finely chopped garlic cloves
1/2 teaspoon finely chopped rosemary
125 ml (4 fl oz/1/2 cup) olive oil

Put the wine into a bowl with the garlic, rosemary and olive oil. Stir to mix. Add your chosen cuts of beef and gently toss so that the pieces are thoroughly coated in the mixture. Put in the refrigerator and marinate for 2–3 hours. Remove the beef from the marinade and season well with freshly ground black pepper. Cook on the barbecue or in a pan until the beef is cooked to your liking. Remove from the heat and season with sea salt. Allow to rest for 5 minutes before serving.

lamb marinade

125 ml (4 fl oz/$^1/_2$ cup) white wine
4 tablespoons olive oil
the juice of 1 lemon
1 tablespoon fresh oregano leaves
1 garlic clove, finely chopped

Put the white wine, olive oil, lemon juice , oregano and garlic into a bowl. Add lamb cutlets, fillets or a boned leg of lamb to the marinade. Toss to thoroughly coat the pieces in the mixture. Marinate in the refrigerator for 2–3 hours. Cook the lamb until it is still a little pink in the centre. Season with sea salt and freshly ground black pepper. Allow to rest for 5 minutes before serving.

rouille

1 thick slice sourdough bread
1 pinch saffron threads
1 red capsicum (pepper), roasted
  and skinned
1/4 teaspoon paprika
2 garlic cloves
125 ml (4 fl oz/1/2 cup) light olive oil

Tear the bread into pieces and put it in a bowl. Bring the saffron threads and 60 ml (1/4 cup) of water to the boil in a small saucepan and simmer for a minute. Pour the hot saffron water over the bread.

Allow the bread to soak in the water and then add it to a food processor or blender with the capsicum, paprika and garlic. Blend to form a smooth paste, then add the olive oil in a stream to give a thick consistency. Season with salt to taste.

caponata

1 large eggplant (aubergine), cut into
  1 cm (1/2 in) dice
60 ml (2 fl oz/1/4 cup) olive oil
1 garlic clove, crushed
1 red capsicum (pepper), finely diced
1 teaspoon thyme leaves
2 tablespoons tomato paste
  (concentrated purée)
1 tablespoon salted capers, rinsed
  and drained
2 tablespoons finely sliced green olives
1 tablespoon finely chopped anchovies
60 g (2 1/4 oz) finely chopped parsley

Lightly salt the eggplant and leave it to drain in a colander for 20 minutes. Rinse and pat dry with paper towels. Heat the oil in a heavy-based saucepan over moderate heat and add the garlic. Stir for 1 minute, then add the eggplant. Cook, stirring occasionally, until the eggplant is lightly golden, then add the capsicum, thyme, tomato paste and 125 ml (4 fl oz/1/2 cup) of water. Reduce the heat and leave to simmer, covered, for 15 minutes, then add the capers, olives and anchovies. Allow to cool. Before serving, fold in the parsley. Serving suggestion.

chilli-lime sauce

makes 200 ml (7 fl oz)

125 g (4^1/$_2$ oz/^{2}/$_3$ cup) grated palm
  sugar (jaggery)
1 tablespoon dried red chilli flakes
2 tablespoons lime juice

Combine the palm sugar with 170 ml (5^1/$_2$ fl oz/^{2}/$_3$ cup) water in a heavy-based saucepan. Bring to the boil and boil for 3 minutes. Add the dried red chilli flakes, stir through, then remove the sauce from the heat. Allow to cool before stirring in the lime juice. Serve with barbecued or baked fish, fresh spring rolls, or drizzled over grilled chicken.

red wine sauce

1 tablespoon red onion, finely diced
1 garlic clove, chopped
2 tablespoons finely chopped celery
2 tablespoons grated carrot
250 ml (9 fl oz/1 cup) red wine
250 ml (9 fl oz/1 cup) veal stock (367)
2 tablespoons chilled diced butter

Put the onion, garlic, celery, carrot and wine in a small saucepan over low heat. Simmer for 10 minutes, then strain into another saucepan and add the veal stock. Bring to the boil, then reduce the heat and simmer for 15 minutes, or until the liquid has been reduced by half. Just before serving, stir or whisk in the butter. Serve with lamb or beef.

shortcrust tart case

makes 1 tart case

200 g (7 oz/1²/₃ cups) plain (all-purpose) flour
100 g (3¹/₂ oz) unsalted butter
1 tablespoon caster (superfine) sugar

Put the flour, butter, sugar and a pinch of salt into a food processor and process for 1 minute. Add 2 tablespoons of chilled water and pulse until the mixture comes together. Wrap the dough in plastic wrap and chill for 30 minutes.

Roll the pastry out as thinly as possible — the easiest way to do this is to roll it out between two layers of plastic wrap. Line a greased 25 cm (10 in) tart tin. Chill for a further 30 minutes. Prick the base, line it with crumpled greaseproof paper and fill with rice or baking weights. Place the tin in a preheated 180°C (350°F/ Gas 4) oven for 10 to 15 minutes or until the pastry looks cooked and dry. Remove and allow to cool.

Note –Tart cases that are not used immediately can be stored in the freezer for several weeks. Put the tart case in a preheated oven direct from the freezer (there's no need to thaw the case first).

shortcrust tartlet cases

makes 36 tartlet cases

200 g (7 oz) plain (all-purpose) flour
100 g (3¹/₂ oz) butter

Put the flour, butter and a pinch of salt into a food processor and process for 1 minute. Add 2 tablespoons of iced water and pulse until the mixture comes together. Wrap in plastic wrap and chill for 30 minutes. Roll the pastry out and cut into rounds. Put into greased patty cake or tartlet tins and chill for a further 30 minutes. Prick the bases and fill with rice or baking weights before placing in a preheated 180°C (350°F/Gas 4) oven for 7–10 minutes. Remove and allow to cool. For a sweet pastry, add 1 tablespoon of caster (superfine) sugar or 1 teaspoon of vanilla extract. Note – Tart shells that are not used immediately can be stored in the freezer for several weeks. Place in a preheated oven direct from the freezer (it is not necessary to thaw the tart shells first).

chocolate icing

250 ml (9 fl oz/1 cup)

100 g (3¹/₂ oz) dark chocolate
125 ml (4 fl oz/¹/₂ cup) thick
  (heavy/double) cream
1 tablespoon Frangelico
1 teaspoon ground cinnamon

To make the icing, put the chocolate and cream into a small saucepan over a very low heat. As the cream begins to get hot, remove the pan from the heat and stir the chocolate until it has melted into the cream to form a thick sauce. Stir in the liqueur and cinnamon and then set the mixture aside to cool a little before icing your cake.

cardamom and rosewater syrup makes 250 ml (9 fl oz/1 cup)

110 g (3³/4 oz/¹/2 cup) sugar
1 teaspoon lemon juice
5 cardamom pods, lightly crushed
¹/2 teaspoon rosewater

Put the sugar, lemon juice and cardamom pods in a small saucepan and add 250 ml (9 fl oz/1 cup) of water. Bring slowly to the boil, making sure that the sugar dissolves completely, then reduce the heat and simmer the mixture for 5 minutes.

Remove the syrup from the heat and stir in the rosewater. This syrup will keep for a couple of weeks in the fridge.

glossary

balsamic vinegar

Balsamic vinegar is a dark, fragrant and sweetish aged vinegar made from grape juice.

basil

The most commonly used basil is the sweet or Genoa variety which is much favoured in Italian cooking. Thai or holy basil is used in Thai and South-East Asian dishes. To get the most out of basil leaves they should always be torn not chopped.

bocconcini

These are small balls of mozzarella, often sold sitting in their own whey. When fresh they are soft and springy to the touch and taste distinctly milky. They are available from most delicatessens.

butter puff pastry

This is puff pastry made with butter rather than vegetable fat, which gives it a much more buttery flavour than standard puff.

capers

Capers are the green buds from a Mediterranean shrub, preserved in brine or salt. Salted capers have a firmer texture and are often smaller than those preserved in brine. Rinse away the brine or salt before using them. Capers are available from good delicatessens.

cardamom

A dried seed pod native to India. The inner seeds when crushed give off a sweet aroma. It is used whole or ground and can be found in the spice section of most supermarkets. Cardamom should be used sparingly, as it is quite strong.

Chinese black beans

These salted black beans can be found either vacuum-packed or in tins in Asian food stores.

chipotle chillies

These are available from delicatessens in tins where they are preserved in a smoky rich sauce, or they can be bought as smoked and dried chillies which need to be reconstituted in warm water prior to use.

chocolate

Couverture is the best quality chocolate to use. This bittersweet chocolate contains the highest percentage of cocoa butter. Available from delicatessens and food stores. If you can't find chocolate of this standard, then use a good-quality eating chocolate.

ciabatta

Italian for 'slipper', this loaf of bread is supposed to be in the shape of a shoe. Very light and with a porous texture, the Italians favour this loaf for sandwiches.

cream

Cream comes with differing fat contents. If it needs to be whipped it must have a fat content higher than 35 per cent. Single and light cream cannot be whipped.

crème fraîche

A naturally soured cream which is lighter than sour cream. it is available at gourmet food stores and some supermarkets.

dried porcini mushrooms

Dried porcini (cep) mushrooms can be found either in small packets or sold loose from a jar in delicatessens.

feta cheese

Feta is a white cheese made from sheep's milk or goat's milk. The cheese is salted and cut into blocks before being matured in its own whey. It must be kept in the whey or in oil during storage. Persian feta is creamy in style. Feta is available from delicatessens and most supermarkets.

Frangelico

A hazelnut-flavoured Italian liqueur sold in a brown bottle shaped like a monk's robe.

goat's curd

This is a soft, fresh cheese made from goat's milk, which has a slightly acidic but mild and creamy flavour.

gruyère cheese

A firm cow's milk cheese with a smooth texture and natural rind. It has a nutty flavour and melts easily, making it perfect for tarts and gratins.

haloumi cheese

Haloumi is a semi-firm sheep's milk cheese. It has a rubbery texture which becomes soft and chewy when the cheese is grilled or fried. It is available from delicatessens and most large supermarkets.

haricot beans

There are many types of beans that belong to the haricot family, including cannellini (kidney-shaped beans) and flageolet (white or pale green beans), and also navy beans, which are famous for their use in baked beans. In Europe and the United States, haricot are also called white beans.

horseradish

Horseradish is the root of the mustard family — large and white, it has a knobbly brown skin. It is very pungent and has a spicy, hot flavour. It is usually freshly grated as a condiment for roast beef and smoked fish. When commercially produced, horseradish is often blended with cream to give it a smoother texture. Dollop on roast beef or smoked salmon.

Indian lime pickle

Lime pickle is available from Indian grocery stores or large supermarkets. It is usually served as a side dish.

jalapeño chillies

Small pickled jalapeño chillies are available in jars in speciality stores and large supermarkets. They add a sweet but fiery bite to salsas and should be used to personal taste.

marsala

Perhaps Italy's most famous fortified wine, Marsala is available in sweet and dry varieties. Often used in desserts such as zabaglione, it is a superb match with eggs, cream and almonds.

mascarpone cheese

This heavy, Italian-style set cream is used as a base in many sweet and savoury dishes. It is made from cream rather than milk, so is high in fat. It is sold at delicatessens and supermarkets.

mozzarella cheese

Fresh mozzarella can be found in most delicatessens and is easily identified by its smooth, white appearance and ball-like shape. It is not to be confused with mass-produced mozzarella, which is mostly used as a pizza topping. Mozzarella is usually sold packed in whey.

mustard seeds

Mustard seeds have a sharp, hot flavour that is tempered by cooking. Both brown and yellow are available, although brown mustard seeds are more common.

niçoise olives

Niçoise or Ligurian olives are small black olives that are used in salads or scattered over dishes. They are not suitable for pitting and making into pastes.

palm sugar

Palm sugar is obtained from the sap of various palm trees and is sold in hard cakes and in plastic jars. If it is very hard it will need to be grated. It can be found in Asian grocery stores or supermarkets.

pancetta

Pancetta is salted belly of pork. It is sold in delicatessens, especially Italian ones, and some supermarkets. Pancetta is available either rolled and thinly sliced or in large pieces ready to be diced or cut. It adds a rich bacon flavour to dishes.

panettone

An aromatic Italian yeast bread made with raisins and candied peel, panettone is traditionally eaten at Christmas, when it is found in Italian delicatessens or large supermarkets. They are available in large and small sizes.

pesto

Available in most supermarkets, pesto is a puréed sauce traditionally made from basil, garlic, Parmesan cheese, pine nuts and olive oil.

pine mushrooms

Also known as matsutake, these Japanese mushrooms are brown in colour and thick and meaty in texture. They are best if cooked simply by sautéeing in butter with a little garlic.

pomegranate molasses

This is a thick syrup made from the reduction of pomegranate juice. It has a bittersweet flavour, which adds a sour bite to many Middle Eastern dishes. It is available from Middle Eastern speciality stores.

preserved lemon

These are whole lemons preserved in salt or brine, which turns their rind soft and pliable. Just the rind is used — the pulp should be scraped out and thrown away. It is available from delicatessens.

prosciutto

Prosciutto is lightly salted, air-dried ham. It is most commonly bought in paper-thin slices, and is available from delicatessens and large supermarkets. Parma ham and San Daniele are both types of prosciutto.

ricotta cheese

Ricotta cheese can be bought cut from a wheel or in tubs. The wheel tends to be firmer in consistency and is better for baking. If you can only get ricotta in tubs, drain off any excess moisture by letting it sit for a couple of hours in a sieve lined with muslin (cheesecloth).

risoni

Risoni are small rice-shaped pasta. They are ideal for use in soups or salads where their small shape is able to absorb the other flavours of the dish.

risotto rice

There are three well-known varieties of risotto rice that are widely available today: arborio, a large plump grain that makes a stickier risotto; vialone nano, a shorter grain that gives a loose consistency but keeps more of a bite in the middle; and carnaroli, similar in size to vialone nano, which makes a risotto with a firm consistency. All are interchangeable, although cooking times may vary by 5 minutes or so.

rosewater

The distilled essence of rose petals, rosewater is used in small quantities to impart a perfumed flavour to pastries, fruit salads and sweet puddings. It is available from delicatessens and large supermarkets.

saffron threads
These are the orange-red stigmas from one species of the crocus plant, and the most expensive spice in the world. Saffron should be bought in small quantities and used sparingly — not only due to the cost but as it has a very strong flavour.

smoked paprika
Paprika is commonly sold as a dried, rich red powder made from a member of the chilli family. It comes in many grades from delicate through to sweet and finally hot. Smoked paprika from Spain adds a distinct rich and smoky flavour.

sour cherries and cherry nectar
These bottled, European-style morello cherries are commonly sold in jars. Both the juice and the fruit are used in cooking. Sour cherry nectar is available in tetra packs from most large supermarkets.

sterilizing jars
It's always a good idea to sterilize jars or bottles before filling with food that you may be intending to keep for a while. To do, wash in hot soapy water, boil for 10 minutes in a large saucepan, then drain on a clean tea towel. Dry in a 130°C (250°F/Gas 1) oven and then remove and fill while the jars are still hot.

tortillas
This thin, round, unleavened bread is used in Mexican cooking as a wrap. Tortillas are available pre-packaged in the refrigerator section of most supermarkets.

truss tomatoes
Truss simply means tomatoes which can be brought on the vine.

vanilla
The long slim black vanilla bean has a wonderful caramel aroma which synthetic vanillas can never capture. Store unused vanilla pods in a full jar of caster (superfine) sugar, which will not only help to keep the vanilla fresh but the aroma of the bean will infuse the sugar, making it ideal for use in baking.

vine leaves
The large, green leaves of the grapevine are available packed in tins, jars or in brine. They are used in Greek and Middle Eastern cookery to wrap foods for cooking. Vine leaves in brine should be rinsed before use.

wonton wrappers
These paper-thin sheets of dough are available fresh or frozen from Asian grocery stores. They can be wrapped around fillings and steamed, deep-fried or used in broths, and come shaped as squares and circles.

index